From the Start

BEGINNING LISTENING

BOOK 1

Jann Huizenga

Longman

TO MY PARENTS

Executive Editor: Joanne Dresner
Project Editor: Penny Laporte
Text Design: Lynn Luchetti
Cover Design: Stephan Zander
Photography: Kim Wm. Crowley
Illustrations: Mary Chandler Martylewski, Nina Tallarico
Production: Eduardo Castillo

From the Start: Beginning Listening Book 1

Longman Inc.
95 Church Street
White Plains, N.Y. 10601

Associated companies:
Longman Group Ltd., London
Longman Cheshire Pty., Melbourne
Longman Paul Pty., Auckland
Copp Clark Pitman, Toronto
Pitman Publishing Inc., New York

Library of Congress Cataloging-in-Publication Data

Huizenga, Jann.
    From the start.

    1. English language—Text-books for foreign speakers.
2. Listening—Problems, exercises, etc. I. Title.
PE1128.H78   1987   428.3'4   86-20016
ISBN   0-582-90727-6 (v. 1)

87 88 89 90 9 8 7 6 5 4 3 2 1

Distributed in the United Kingdom by Longman
Group Ltd., Longman House, Burnt Mill, Harlow,
Essex CM20 2JE, England, and by associated
companies, branches, and representatives
throughout the world.

Printed in the U.S.A.

CONTENTS

INTRODUCTION

From the Start is a photograph-based listening comprehension text intended for students who have had little or no exposure to spoken or written English.

The material has been written with several goals in mind. One is to provide students with truly "comprehensible input", i.e., an acquisition stage in which a high degree of contextualization would allow them to formulate hypotheses and discover meaning in language they are hearing for the first time. Thus the workbook and tape include a presentation stage in which the new language on tape is contextualized not only by its situational authenticity but by its exact correspondence with a series of photographs in the student's book. The extra-linguistic context is seen as crucial in helping students at this level to understand and acquire. Another goal of the material is to give students ample opportunity to test their new hypotheses. Therefore, the *Focus* exercises are designed to allow students to verify their comprehension in a simple, non-verbal fashion. Finally, the material aims to give students a chance to listen to language and absorb it before producing it. Production is thus delayed until the end of each unit, where optional production activities can be found.

Each of the 16 units begins with a brief, contextualized dialogue establishing the setting and associated language or functions. Early units, for example, introduce numbers in the context of a bank (counting dollar bills) and directory assistance (asking for addresses and telephone numbers). Later units present functions such as requesting information or giving directions. As students listen to the conversation on tape, they follow along in the workbook with a series of photographs representing the word or phrase they are hearing. In the *Focus* section, students receive feedback on their comprehension through tasks in which they respond non-verbally: by circling, numbering, checking, matching, or drawing. They then progress to recognition of written forms. For students who are ready to produce, the *Follow Up* section at the end of each unit provides oral and written production tasks.

USING THE TEXT

Before playing the presentation on tape, give your students a minute to look at the overview photo, which will make the general setting clear, and then at the rest of the photos, which will clarify the particular topics. Briefly previewing in this manner will allow students to predict what is coming and thus to relax and better comprehend. The presentation occurs twice on the tape, the first time with the narrator interjecting the numbers of the photos to assure that students make the correct correspondence between language utterance and photo. The second time is without the narrator. If your students want to listen again, rewind and play the tape as many times as necessary. The *Focus* section consists of three or four listening tasks, all requiring non-verbal responses to recorded material. The first provides feedback to students on how well they have understood and internalized the language in the presentation. The next introduces students to the written form of what they have heard. The following one or two tasks allow students to test their comprehension of the language in a recombined form or in a slightly different context. Students may need to listen to an exercise more than once. Each exercise should be checked immediately after it is completed since the exercises build upon each other. A good way to do this is to elicit answers from students and then replay the exercise once or twice. This will allow students with incorrect answers to better understand the source of their errors. A perforated answer key is found at the back of the text. The optional *Follow Up* activities require production and are not on tape. The tasks include oral information gap activities for pair work, and limited writing tasks.

ACKNOWLEDGEMENTS

Special thanks to my husband Kim for taking on the onerous task of the photography, and to our families, friends, colleagues, and students for posing for the photographs. My colleagues at LaGuardia Community College have provided much of the inspiration for this text, and I thank them for sharing their ideas. At Longman, thanks are due to Penny Laporte, Project Editor, for the loving care she gave a most difficult manuscript; to Joanne Dresner, Executive Editor, for her inspiration and boundless energy; to Lynn Luchetti and Stephan Zander, Designers; and to Arthur Custer, Audio Producer. The help of reviewers Carol Numrich, Elizabeth Tannenbaum, and K. Lynn Savage is also much appreciated.

Look at the pictures and listen.

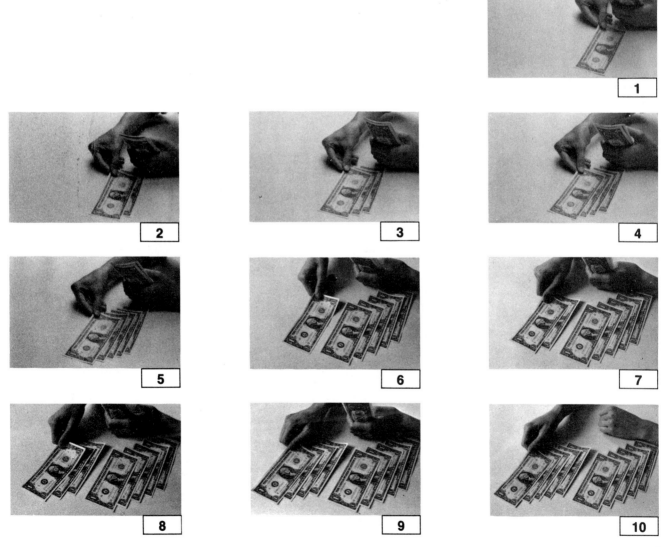

FOCUS

Exercise 1

Listen and circle the number you hear.

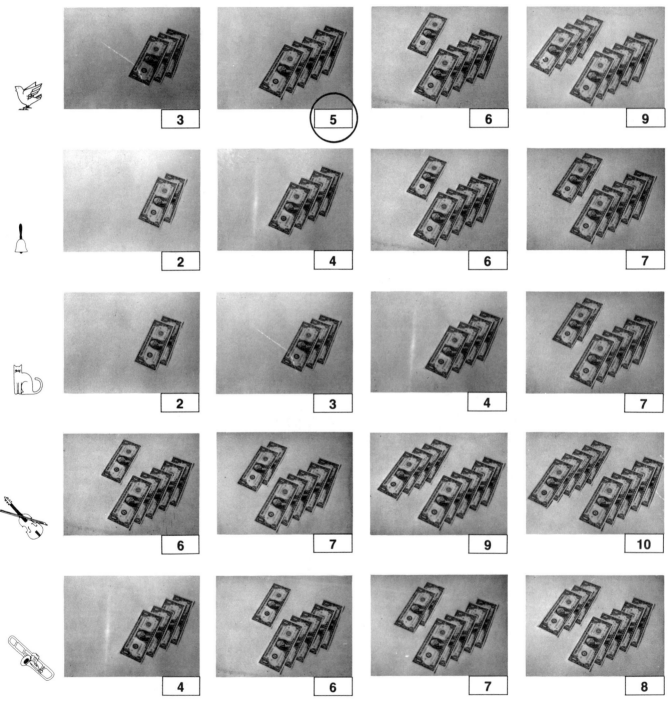

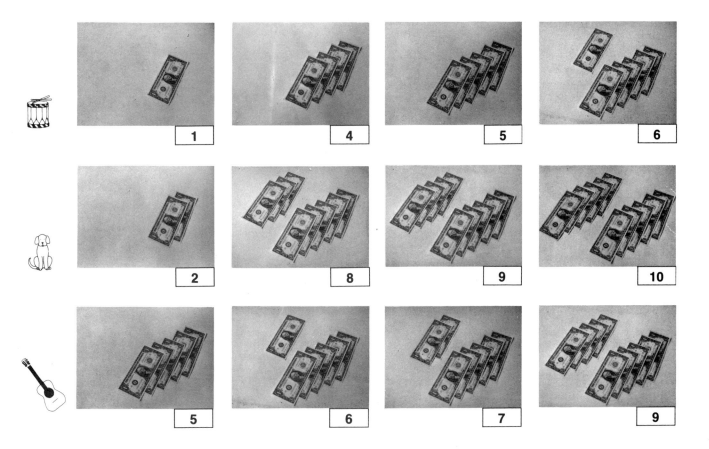

Exercise 2

Listen and write the number you hear.

🐦	_____8_____	🎺	_____
🔔	_____	🥁	_____
🐈	_____	🐕	_____
🎻	_____	🎸	_____

Exercise 3

Look at the words and listen.

one
two
three
four
five
six
seven
eight
nine
ten

Exercise 4

Listen and circle the word you hear.

	(six)	one	three	seven
	two	ten	one	three
	eight	one	nine	ten
	four	five	nine	six
	six	five	seven	nine
	three	two	ten	eight

4 four

FOLLOW UP

Exercise 5

Work with a partner.
Student A reads a number.
Student B circles the number.
Student A looks at the number. Is it the right one?

Now Student B reads a number.
Student A circles the number.

		1	2	3	4	5	6	7	8	9	10
1.	STUDENT A SPEAKS: *STUDENT B WRITES.*	1	2	3	4	5	6	7	8	9	10
2.	STUDENT B SPEAKS: *STUDENT A WRITES.*	1	2	3	4	5	6	7	8	9	10
3.	STUDENT A:	1	2	3	4	5	6	7	8	9	10
4.	STUDENT B:	1	2	3	4	5	6	7	8	9	10
5.	STUDENT A:	1	2	3	4	5	6	7	8	9	10
6.	STUDENT B:	1	2	3	4	5	6	7	8	9	10
7.	STUDENT A:	1	2	3	4	5	6	7	8	9	10
8.	STUDENT B:	1	2	3	4	5	6	7	8	9	10
9.	STUDENT A:	1	2	3	4	5	6	7	8	9	10
10.	STUDENT B:	1	2	3	4	5	6	7	8	9	10

Exercise 6

Write the numbers.

1 one

2

3

4

5

6

7

8

9

10

Look at the pictures and listen.

1.

FOO CHOW
Restaurant
1273 THIRD AVE.

626-2834

2.

LEGAL AID

577-3301

Main Office:
182 Church St.

3.

PARK HOSPITAL

PRIVATE HOSPITAL
19 Park Ave.
between Green St. and Hudson Ave.

CALL
828-7887

4.

HOTEL
George Washington

250-4932

LEXINGTON AVE. AT 23rd ST.

5.

TRANS WORLD AIRLINES

THE U.S.,
EUROPE AND
THE MIDDLE EAST   **TWA**

"FOR INFORMATION CALL"

691-2303

6.

CITY BANK

• All Services •
587-5160

• Head Office: One Wall Plaza
• Branches:
   203 Fulton Road
   98 South Main Street

FOCUS

Exercise 1

Listen and circle the number you hear.

 536-4212   (536-4202)

 345-9762   345-9752

 454-8976   454-9976

 778-2056   778-2046

 626-1139   636-1139

 255-7509   251-7509

782-3386   872-3386

871-0402   871-0482

Exercise 2

Listen and write the missing numbers.

 5 _9_ _8_ -3257

 289- ___ ___ 82

 742-62 ___ ___

 ___ ___ 5-7160

357- ___ ___ 22

 652-27 ___ ___

 4 ___ ___ -7045

 921- ___ ___ 38

Exercise 3

Listen and write the number you hear.

 _462-8069_

 _____

 _____

_____

 _____

 _____

 _____

_____

FOLLOW UP

Exercise 4

Work with a partner.
Student A reads a number.
Student B circles the number.
Student A looks at the number. Is it the right one?

Now Student B reads a number.
Student A circles the number.

1. STUDENT A SPEAKS: 636-2789   646-2789   636-2798
   STUDENT B WRITES.

2. STUDENT B SPEAKS: 331-9045   339-9045   339-9145
   STUDENT A WRITES.

3. STUDENT A: 528-5618   528-5668   528-5688

4. STUDENT B: 788-1175   788-1165   688-1165

5. STUDENT A: 945-2167   945-3167   945-3177

6. STUDENT B: 626-4802   636-4802   626-4892

7. STUDENT A: 423-3597   423-3596   423-3059

8. STUDENT B: 988-2864   989-2864   988-2064

Unit

3

Change for
a twenty,
please.

Look at the pictures and listen.

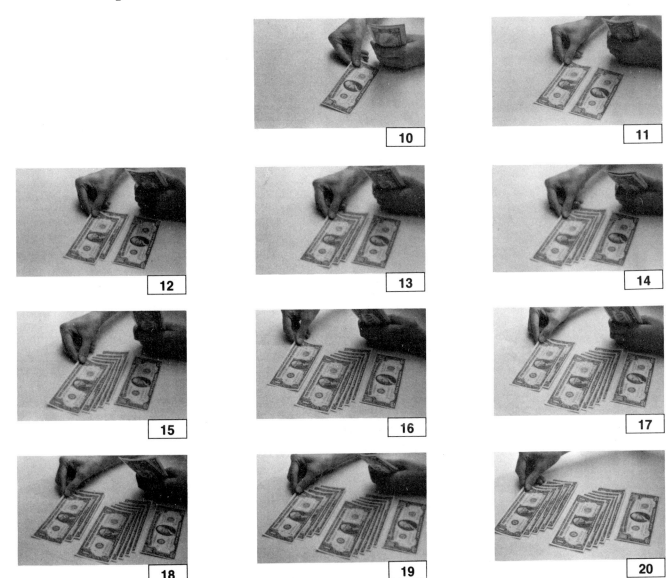

10

11

12

13

14

15

16

17

18

19

20

FOCUS

Exercise 1

Listen and circle the number you hear.

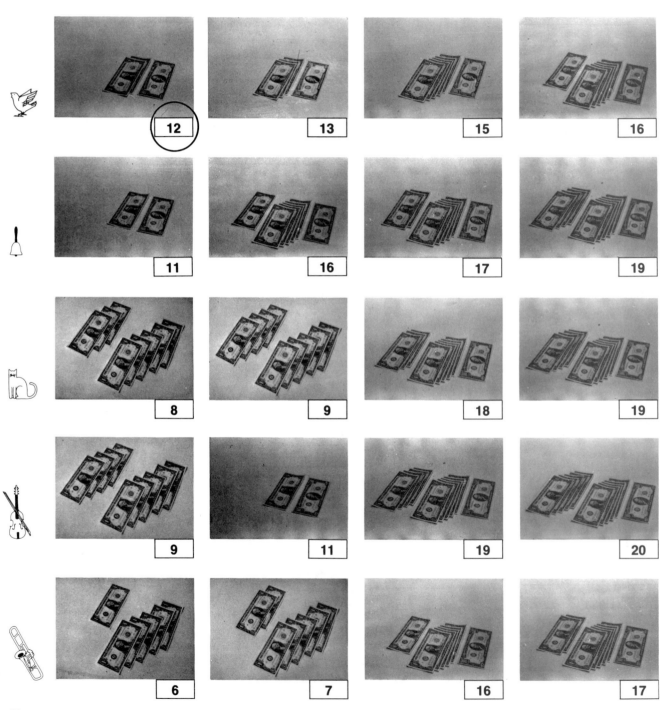

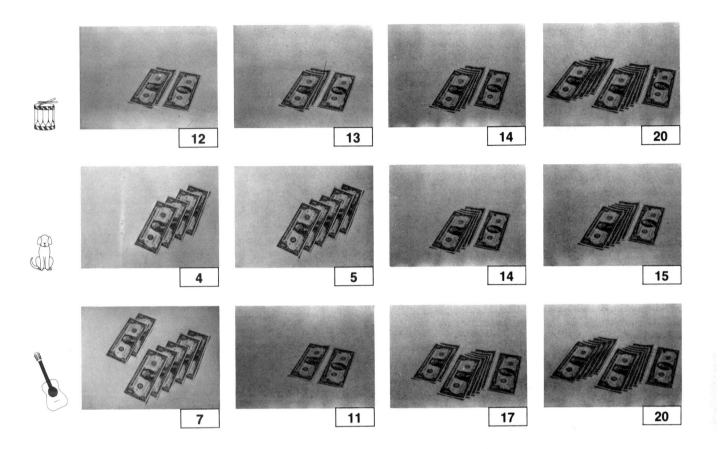

Exercise 2

Listen and write the number you hear.

🕊️	12	🎺	
🔔		🥁	
🐱		🐶	
🎻		🎸	

Exercise 3

Look at the words and listen.

eleven
twelve
thirteen
fourteen
fifteen
sixteen
seventeen
eighteen
nineteen
twenty

Exercise 4

Listen and circle the word you hear.

fourteen	fifteen	(sixteen)	seventeen
eleven	eighteen	eight	one
six	seven	sixteen	seventeen
twenty	twelve	three	thirteen
fourteen	fifteen	four	five
eight	nine	eighteen	nineteen

FOLLOW UP

Exercise 5

Work with a partner.
Student A reads a number.
Student B circles the number.
Student A looks at the number. Is it the right one?

Now Student B reads a number.
Student A circles the number.

1.	STUDENT A SPEAKS: *STUDENT B WRITES.*	11	12	13	14	15	16	17	18
2.	STUDENT B SPEAKS: *STUDENT A WRITES.*	5	7	9	11	13	15	17	19
3.	STUDENT A:	1	2	3	4	5	6	7	8
4.	STUDENT B:	10	11	12	13	17	18	19	20
5.	STUDENT A:	12	13	14	15	16	17	18	19
6.	STUDENT B:	7	8	9	10	11	12	13	14
7.	STUDENT A:	1	2	3	4	11	12	13	20
8.	STUDENT B:	7	8	9	10	17	18	19	20
9.	STUDENT A:	2	3	4	5	12	13	14	15
10.	STUDENT B:	12	13	14	15	16	17	18	19

Exercise 6

Write the numbers.

11 _eleven_   16 _____

12 _____   17 _____

13 _____   18 _____

14 _____   19 _____

15 _____   20 _____

Unit 4

Ten tens, please.

Look at the pictures and listen.

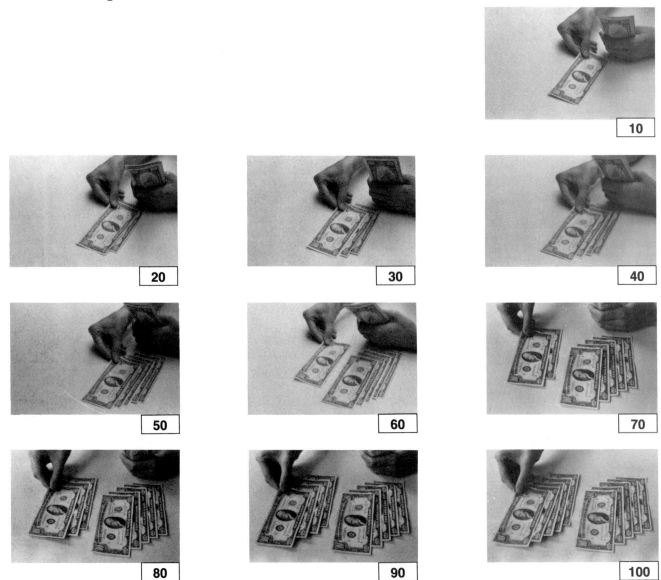

10

20

30

40

50

60

70

80

90

100

FOCUS

Exercise 1

Listen and circle the number you hear.

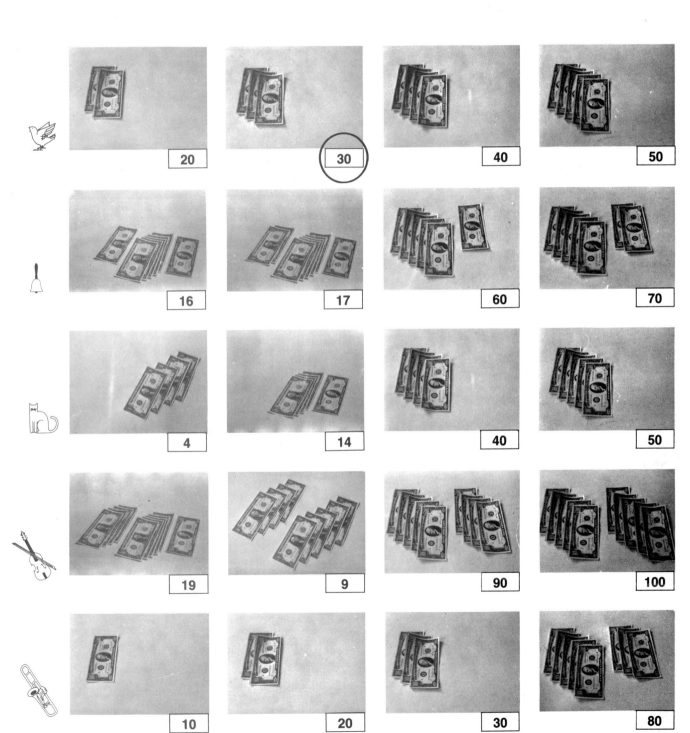

	20	(30)	40	50
	16	17	60	70
	4	14	40	50
	19	9	90	100
	10	20	30	80

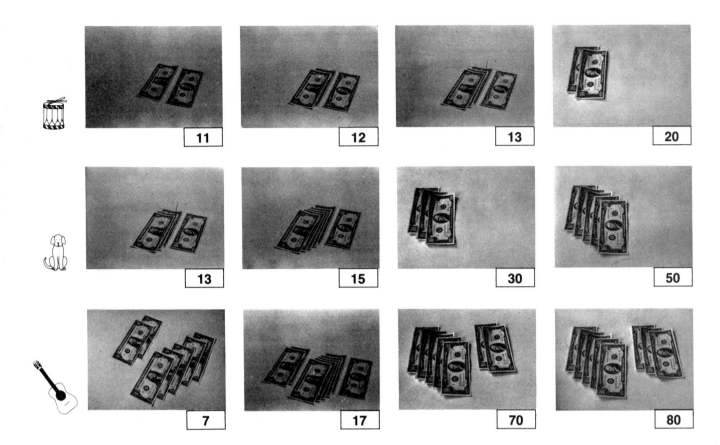

Exercise 2

Listen and write the number you hear.

70

Exercise 3

Look at the words and listen.

ten
twenty
thirty
forty
fifty
sixty
seventy
eighty
ninety
one hundred

Exercise 4

Listen and circle the word you hear.

four   fourteen   (forty)   fifty

seventeen   seventy   eleven   sixteen

eighty   ninety   nineteen   nine

thirty   twenty   twelve   thirteen

six   sixteen   sixty   seventy

two   ten   twenty   thirty

FOLLOW UP

Exercise 5

Work with a partner.
Student A reads a number.
Student B circles the number.
Student A looks at the number. Is it the right one?

Now Student B reads a number.
Student A circles the number.

1.	STUDENT A SPEAKS: *STUDENT B WRITES.*	10	20	30	40	50	60	70	80	90	100
2.	STUDENT B SPEAKS: *STUDENT A WRITES.*	10	20	30	40	50	60	70	80	90	100
3.	STUDENT A:	13	14	15	16	17	30	40	50	60	70
4.	STUDENT B:	13	14	15	16	17	30	40	50	60	70
5.	STUDENT A:	2	3	4	12	13	14	20	30	40	
6.	STUDENT B:	2	3	4	12	13	14	20	30	40	
7.	STUDENT A:	1	9	10	11	18	19	80	90	100	
8.	STUDENT B:	1	9	10	11	18	19	80	90	100	
9.	STUDENT A:	12	20	30	40	50	60	70	80	90	100
10.	STUDENT B:	12	20	30	40	50	60	70	80	90	100

Exercise 6

Write the numbers.

10	ten	60	_____
20	_____	70	_____
30	_____	80	_____
40	_____	90	_____
50	_____	100	_____

Unit 5

What's your address?

Look at the pictures and listen.

1.

2.

3.

4.

5.

6.

7.

8.

FOCUS

Exercise 1

Listen and circle the address you hear.

1. 655 State Street   (665 State Street)

2. 82 East Avenue   83 East Avenue

3. 428 Pine Street   448 Pine Street

4. 144 Spring Road   1404 Spring Road

5. 139 Lake Avenue   129 Lake Avenue

6. 5206 Main Street   5026 Main Street

7. 5790 Elm Street   5719 Elm Street

8. 4304 Lincoln Avenue   434 Lincoln Avenue

Exercise 2

Listen and write the missing numbers.

1. 3 _2_ _5_ South Street

2. 12 _ _ _ _ Brook Avenue

3. _ _ _ _ 1 Bay Road

4. _ _ _ _ 68 Grand Avenue

5. 76 _ _ _ _ First Street

6. 5 _ _ _ _ River Road

7. _ _ _ _ 92 Madison Avenue

8. 2 _ _ _ _ Mountain Lane

Exercise 3

Listen and write the address you hear.

1. _742_ Main Street

2. _____ Linden Avenue

3. _____ Church Road

4. _____ Oak Street

5. _____ Penfield Road

6. _____ Lake Avenue

FOLLOW UP

Exercise 4

Work with a partner.
Student A reads an address.
Student B circles the address.
Student A looks at the address. Is it the right one?

Now Student B reads an address.
Student A circles the address.

1. STUDENT A SPEAKS: 428 Bush Street   4028 Bush Street   408 Bush Street
   STUDENT B WRITES.

2. STUDENT B SPEAKS: 7209 Jackson Street   7029 Jackson Street   1729 Jackson Street
   STUDENT A WRITES.

3. STUDENT A: 508 West Avenue   58 West Avenue   580 West Avenue

4. STUDENT B: 177 Glen Road   1707 Glen Road   1007 Glen Road

5. STUDENT A: 1384 Park Avenue   3084 Park Avenue   1394 Park Avenue

6. STUDENT B: 219 Spring Road   209 Spring Road   290 Spring Road

7. STUDENT A: 2880 Hill Street   2808 Hill Street   2080 Hill Street

8. STUDENT B: 1560 East Avenue   5060 East Avenue   1516 East Avenue

Exercise 5

Work with a partner.
Student A says his or her address.
Student B writes the address.
Student A looks at the address. Is it right?

Now Student B says his or her address.
Student A writes the address.

Your name, please.

 Look at the pictures and listen.

1. Mr. Dinn

2. Mrs. Rindell

3. Mr. Reid

4. Mr. Soleri

5. Mrs. Flores

6. Ms. Toledo

7. Mr. Westoff

8. Miss Ferrings

9. Mr. Konikow

10. Mrs. Krieger

FOCUS

Exercise 1

Listen and write the missing letter.

1. Dw ___i___ re
   (o,e,i)

2. _____ odin
   (I,R,L)

3. N _____ lson
   (i,o,e)

4. Gor _____ on
   (e,t,d)

5. Fen _____
   (d,g,k)

6. Wei _____
   (l,o,r)

7. K _____ tts
   (o,e,i)

8. _____ inger
   (S,F,W)

9. Lan _____
   (g,e,i)

10. Fos _____ er
    (d,i,t)

Exercise 2

Listen and circle the name you hear.

1. (Dine)	Tine	Dile	Dein
2. Senn	Fenn	Fonn	Feno
3. Gint	Gene	Dent	Gent
4. Leef	Leff	Lief	Liff
5. Keer	Keel	Keil	Keen
6. Ting	Deng	Ding	Teng
7. Fein	Finn	Fern	Feir
8. Stole	Stoll	Stolt	Stold

Exercise 3

Listen and write the missing letter.

1. L _e_ on

2. Dre ____

3. Fi ____ ler

4. Kelle ____

5. Dod ____ e

6. ____ ton

7. G ____ ll

8. Fe ____ d

9. Rot ____ in

10. Tilso ____

Exercise 4

Listen and write the names.

1. Ford _____

2. _____

3. _____

4. _____

5. _____

6. _____

7. _____

8. _____

9. _____

10. _____

FOLLOW UP

Exercise 5

Work with a partner.
Student A spells a name.
Student B circles the name.
Student A looks at the name. Is it the right one?

Now Student B spells a name.
Student A circles the name.

1. STUDENT A SPEAKS: | Lose | Rose | Ross | Losk |
   STUDENT B WRITES.

2. STUDENT B SPEAKS: Grose   Gries   Gress   Gross
   STUDENT A WRITES.

3. STUDENT A: | Fein | Finn | Fine | Feen |

4. STUDENT B: Stern   Stone   Stein   Steen

5. STUDENT A: | Feng | Fing | Fend | Fine |

6. STUDENT B: Winn   Weir   Wein   Wenn

7. STUDENT A: | Groff | Griff | Grigg | Grife |

8. STUDENT B: Kent   King   Kind   Kirt

9. STUDENT A: | Tieng | Tighe | Tiden | Ting |

10. STUDENT B: Klose   Kroff   Kross   Kloss

SOCIAL SECURITY

Spell it, please.

Look at the pictures and listen.

1. Mrs. Chan

2. Mr. Zachary

3. Mrs. Jacoby

4. Mr. Zimmer

5. Mr. Buxton

6. Ms. Ajax

7. Mrs. Quincy

8. Mr. Paquette

9. Mrs. Mavis

10. Mr. Pavlov

FOCUS

Exercise 1

Listen and write the missing letter.

1. Bea __n__ e
   (m,n,l)

2. M _____ ller
   (i,o,u)

3. _____ hang
   (C,Z,S)

4. Co _____ en
   (a,h,w)

5. _____ oss
   (V,B,P)

6. Mo _____ ey
   (x,s,z)

7. _____ iles
   (J,G,Z)

8. B _____ er
   (i,y,a)

9. L _____ vy
   (i,e,a)

10. Hai _____ e
    (l,r,n)

Exercise 2

Listen and circle the name you hear.

1. Becker	Becher	(Bacher)	Baker
2. Felix	Feliz	Files	Filix
3. Kohan	Kowan	Koven	Kogen
4. Shen	Chen	Chan	Zhen
5. Parker	Barker	Parkin	Barkin
6. Mohr	Mohl	Moor	Moar
7. Gant	Jant	Gans	Ganz
8. Majer	Mayer	Maier	Major

Exercise 3

Listen and write the missing letter.

1. Shar _p_

2. ___ nger

3. R ___ an

4. ___ urphy

5. Di ___ on

6. Sta ___ l

7. De ___ lin

8. Na ___ ler

9. W ___ ner

10. Ari ___ a

Exercise 4

Listen and write the names.

1. James

2. ___

3. ___

4. ___

5. ___

6. ___

7. ___

8. ___

9. ___

10. ___

FOLLOW UP

Exercise 5

Work with a partner.
Student A spells a name.
Student B circles the name.
Student A looks at the name. Is it the right one?

Now Student B spells a name.
Student A circles the name.

1.	STUDENT A SPEAKS: *STUDENT B WRITES.*	Bower	Bauer	Bowen	Bawer
2.	STUDENT B SPEAKS: *STUDENT A WRITES.*	Jaffe	Goffe	Yoffe	Joffe
3.	STUDENT A:	Ryder	Rider	Rieder	Reder
4.	STUDENT B:	Mogul	Mogil	Mogel	Mogal
5.	STUDENT A:	Visser	Visher	Wisser	Wiser
6.	STUDENT B:	Brenner	Brendel	Brender	Brenden
7.	STUDENT A:	Zachs	Sachs	Zacks	Sacks
8.	STUDENT B:	Grazi	Grace	Graze	Graci
9.	STUDENT A:	Feld	Felt	Fert	Fell
10.	STUDENT B:	Hanes	Hines	Haynes	Haines

Exercise 6

Work with a partner.
Student A spells his or her name.
Student B writes the name.
Student A looks at the name. Is it right?

Now Student B spells his or her name.
Student A writes the name.

_____ (first name) _____ (last name)

What would you like to eat?

Look at the pictures and listen.

1.

2.

3.

4.

5.

6.

7.

8.

9.

10.

11.

12.

FOCUS

Exercise 1

Listen to the questions. Match the questions with the pictures.

_____

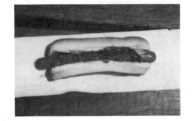

_____

1

_____

_____

_____

Exercise 2

Listen to the questions. Match the questions with the pictures.

_____

_____

_____

_____

1

_____

Exercise 3

Listen to the customers. Circle the food they order.

1.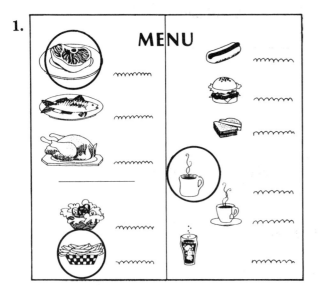

2.

3.

4.

Exercise 4

Number the questions as you hear them.

_____ Coke?   _____ Water?

_____ A steak?   _____ Chicken?

_____ Milk?   _____ French fries?

_____ A hamburger?   _____ A sandwich?

_____ A salad?   _____ A hot dog?

__1__ Fish?   _____ A milkshake?

Exercise 5

Complete the conversations.

fish   chicken   Coke   tea
hot dog   salad   milk   coffee

1. WAITER: What would you like to eat?

   WOMAN: I'd like a chicken sandwich, a _salad_ and a _____ , please.

2. WAITER: OK. And what would you like?

   CHILD: I'd like a _____ and french fries.

   WAITER: And to drink?

   CHILD: _____ , please.

3. WAITER: Sir?

   MAN: The _____ , please.

   WAITER: Anything to drink?

   MAN: _____ and some water.

4. WAITER: OK. What would you like ma'am?

   WOMAN: _____ and french fries, please. And _____ .

FOLLOW UP

Exercise 6

Work with a partner.
Student A is a waiter.
Student B looks at the menu and orders.
Student A circles the food on the menu.
Student B looks at the menu. Is it the right food?

Now Student B is the waiter.
Student A orders.
Student B circles the food on the menu.

1.   WAITER (STUDENT A):   What would
   you like?

      CUSTOMER (STUDENT B):   . . . .

2.   WAITER (STUDENT B):   . . . . ?
      CUSTOMER (STUDENT A): . . . .

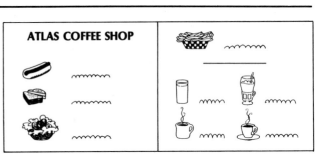

3.   WAITER (STUDENT A):   . . . . ?
      CUSTOMER (STUDENT B): . . . .

4.   WAITER (STUDENT B):   . . . . ?
      CUSTOMER (STUDENT A): . . . .

5.   WAITER (STUDENT A):   . . . . ?
      CUSTOMER (STUDENT B): . . . .

6.   WAITER (STUDENT B):   . . . . ?
      CUSTOMER (STUDENT A): . . . .

Exercise 7

Write the name of the food in each picture.

1.  chicken _____

2. _____

3. _____

4. _____

5. _____

6. _____

7. _____

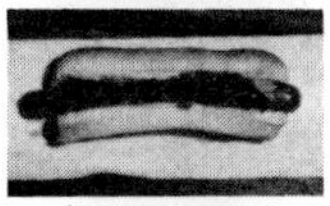

8. _____

9. _____

10. _____

11. _____

12. _____

13. _____

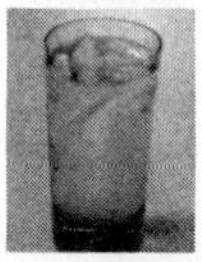

14. _____

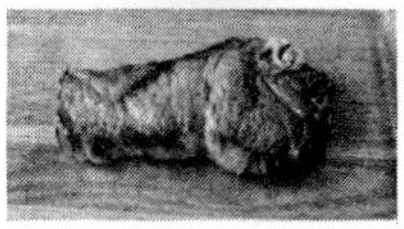

Tell us about the apartment.

Look at the pictures and listen.

1.

2.

3.

4.

5.

6.

7.

8.

FOCUS

Exercise 1

Listen to the sentences. Match the sentences with the pictures.

_____

_____

_____

_____

_____

_____

_____

Exercise 2

Listen to the conversation. Does the apartment have the item in the picture? Circle *yes* or *no*.

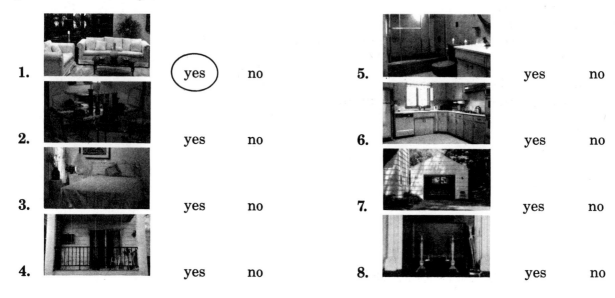

1. (yes)   no
2. yes   no
3. yes   no
4. yes   no

5. yes   no
6. yes   no
7. yes   no
8. yes   no

Exercise 3

Number the sentences as you hear them.

_____ Oh! And there's a balcony.

_____ Is there a garage?

_____ Well, there's a living room.

__1__ Tell us about the apartment.

_____ No, there isn't a fireplace.

_____ There's one bedroom.

_____ Is there a fireplace?

_____ There's a kitchen, a dining room and one bathroom.

_____ No, there isn't.

FOLLOW UP

Exercise 4

Work with a partner.
Student A describes his or her home.
Student B asks questions about the home (*Is there a . . . ?*) and draws a plan.
Student A looks at the plan. Is it right?

Now Student B describes his or her home.
Student A asks questions and draws a plan.

PLAN

Balcony	Dining room
	Fireplace
	Living room
Garage	Kitchen
	Bathroom	Bedroom

YOUR PARTNER'S HOME

Exercise 5

Write a sentence about each picture.

1.  _There isn't a kitchen._

2.  _There's a bedroom._

3. _____

4. _____

5. _____

6. _____

7. _____

8. _____

I need your name.

Look at the pictures and listen.

1.

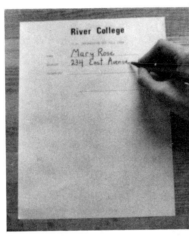

2.

3.

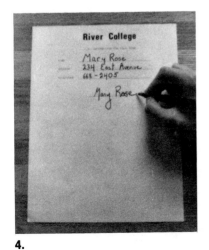

4.

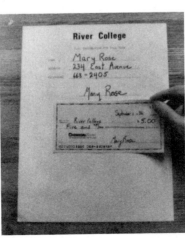

5.

6.

FOCUS

Exercise 1

Circle the item you hear.

1.  | Mary Rose | 234 East Avenue | 668-2405 |

2.  | Mary Rose | Mary Rose | 668-2405 |

3. | 234 East Avenue |  | 668-2405 | Mary Rose |

4.  | | | Mary Rose |

5. | | Mary Rose | 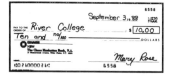 | 234 East Avenue |

6. | 234 East Avenue |  | 668-2405 | 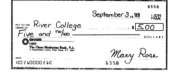 |

7.  | 668-2405 | Mary Rose | Mary Rose |

8. | 234 East Avenue | 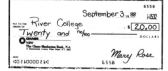 |  | 668-2405 |

Exercise 2

Number the sentences as you hear them.

_____ I need a check for $50.   _____ Thank you.

_____ Here.   _____ And your name and phone number.

_____ And a photograph.   _____ OK.

___1___ I need your address.   _____ Your signature.

Exercise 3

Listen and circle the sentence you hear.

1. **a.** I need a check for $10 and a photograph.
    b. I need a check for $5 and a photograph.
    c. I need a check and a photograph.

2. **a.** I need your phone number, name and address.
    b. I need your phone number and address.
    c. I need a photograph and your address.

3. **a.** I need your name and phone number.
    b. I need your name and a photograph.
    c. I need your name and signature.

4. **a.** I need your phone number and a check for $15.
    b. I need your phone number and signature.
    c. I need a photograph and a check for $50.

5. **a.** I need your signature, name and address.
    b. I need your signature and address.
    c. I need your signature and your check.

6. **a.** I need a check for $25, and your name and address.
    b. I need a check for $35, and your name and address.
    c. I need your signature, and your name and address.

FOLLOW UP

Exercise 4

Work with a partner.
Student A names the items he or she needs.
Student B circles the items.
Student A looks at the items. Are they the right ones?

Now Student B names the items he or she needs.
Student A circles the items.

1. STUDENT A SPEAKS:
   STUDENT B WRITES.

   I need your . . . . and . . . .

   | Mary Rose | Mary Rose | 668-2405 | 234 East Avenue |

2. STUDENT B SPEAKS:
   STUDENT A WRITES.

   I need a . . . . and a . . . .

   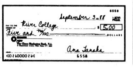  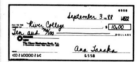 Ana Tanaka

3. STUDENT A:

   I need your . . . . and . . . .

   | 933-7054 | 68 Main Street | Ana Tanaka | Ana Tanaka |

4. STUDENT B:

   I need a . . . . and a . . . .

5. STUDENT A:

   I need your . . . . and . . . .

    Robert Jones  39 Maple Avenue

6. STUDENT B:

   I need your . . . . and . . . .

   | Robert Jones | 39 Maple Avenue | Robert Jones | 761-9004 |

How much is this shampoo?

Look at the pictures and listen.

$1.79

1.

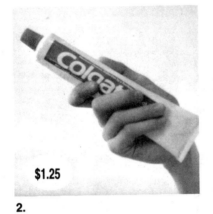

$1.25

2.

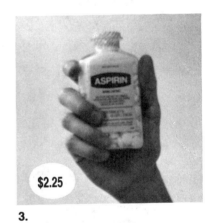

$2.25

3.

$3.09

4.

$5.60

5.

$1.30

6.

FOCUS

Exercise 1

Circle the item and the price you hear.

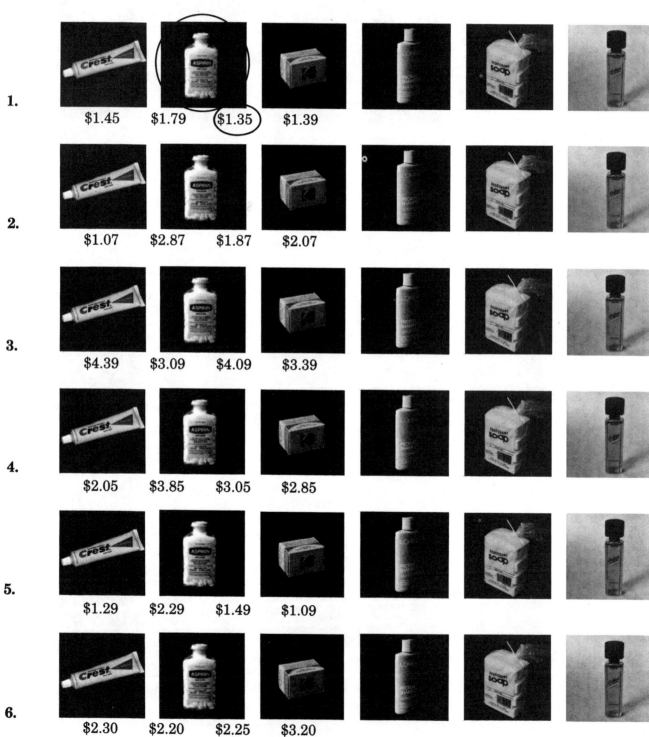

1. $1.45 $1.79   ($1.35) $1.39

2. $1.07 $2.87 $1.87 $2.07

3. $4.39 $3.09 $4.09 $3.39

4. $2.05 $3.85 $3.05 $2.85

5. $1.29 $2.29 $1.49 $1.09

6. $2.30 $2.20 $2.25 $3.20

Exercise 2

Number the sentences as you hear them.

_____ How much is this shampoo?

_____ How much is this cologne?

_____ How much is this aspirin?

__1__ How much is this film?

_____ How much is this toothpaste?

_____ How much is this soap?

Exercise 3

Listen and write the missing number.

1. It's $1._O_5.

2. It's $___.87.

3. It's $4.___5.

4. It's $___.99

5. It's $3.0___.

6. It's $2.___6.

7. It's $___.27.

8. It's $2.___0.

Exercise 4

Listen and write the price you hear.

1. $1.60

2. _____

3. _____

4. _____

5. _____

6. _____

7. _____

8. _____

9. _____

10. _____

FOLLOW UP

Exercise 5

Work with a partner.
Student A asks the price of an item.
Student B reads a price.
Student A circles the price.
Student B looks at the price. Is it the right one?

Now Student B asks the price of an item
Student A reads a price.
Student B circles the price.

1. STUDENT A: How much is this toothpaste?

   $2.90 $2.19   ($2.09) $2.99

   STUDENT B: It's $2.09.

2. STUDENT B: . . . . ?

   $2.17 $2.70 $3.70 $2.60

   STUDENT A: . . . .

3. STUDENT A: . . . . ?

   $1.76 $1.67 $1.70 $1.07

   STUDENT B: . . . .

4. STUDENT B: .... ?

              $1.15 $1.50 $1.05 $1.55

    STUDENT A: ....

5. STUDENT A: .... ?

              $4.88 $4.80 $4.90 $4.98

    STUDENT B: ....

Exercise 6

Write the name of the item in each picture.

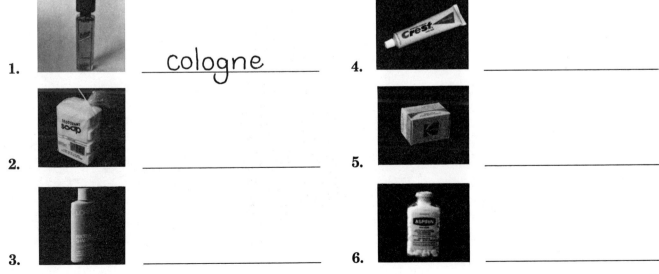

1. cologne

2. _____

3. _____

4. _____

5. _____

6. _____

How much are these vitamins?

Look at the pictures and listen.

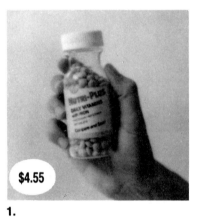

$4.55

1.

85¢

2.

$ .98

3.

67¢

4.

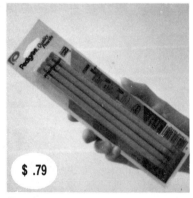

$ .79

5.

$1.19

6.

FOCUS

Exercise 1

Circle the item and the price you hear.

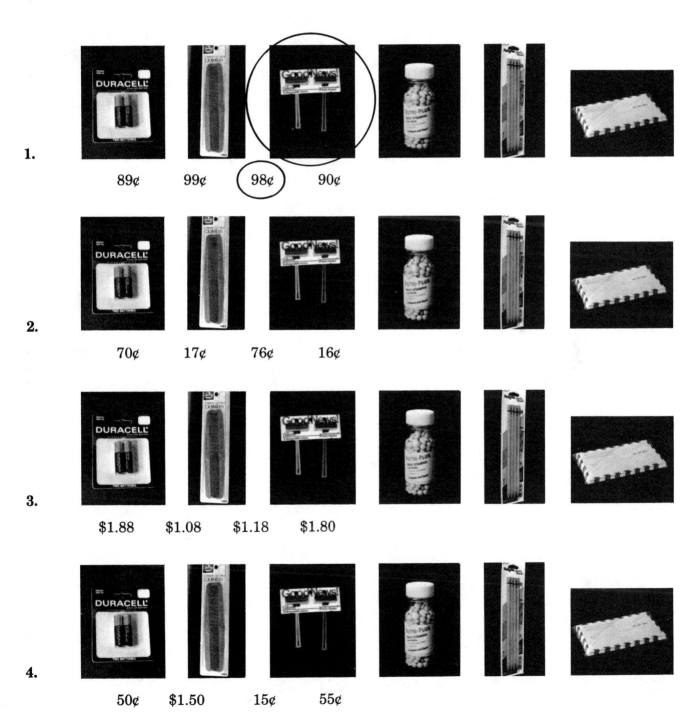

1.
89¢   99¢   98¢   90¢

2.
70¢   17¢   76¢   16¢

3.
$1.88 $1.08 $1.18 $1.80

4.
50¢ $1.50   15¢   55¢

5.

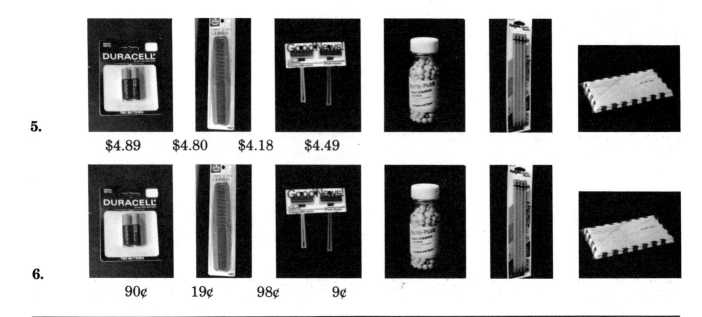

$4.89 $4.80 $4.18 $4.49

6.

90¢   19¢   98¢   9¢

Exercise 2

Listen and circle the item or items in each conversation.

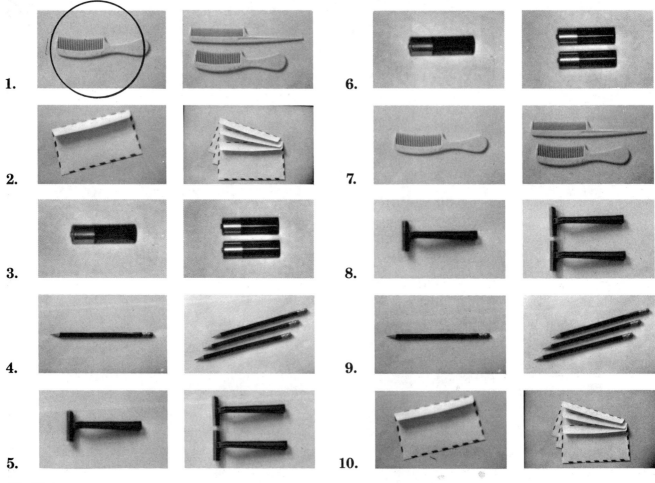

Exercise 3

Number the sentences as you hear them.

_____	They're $2.00.	_____	It's $1.00.
_____	How much is this comb?	_____	How much are these batteries?
_____	How much is this battery?	___1___	How much are these envelopes?
_____	They're $1.00.	_____	It's $.50.

Exercise 4

Complete the conversations.

comb	razor	vitamins	batteries
combs	razors	toothpaste	soap

1. CUSTOMER: Pardon me. How much are these __vitamins__ ?
    CLERK: They're $3.00.
    CUSTOMER: And how much is this _____ ?
    CLERK: It's $.75.
    CUSTOMER: Thanks.

2. CUSTOMER: Excuse me. How much is this _____ ?
    CLERK: It's $1.30.
    CUSTOMER: And these _____ ?
    CLERK: $1.50.

3. CUSTOMER: How much is this _____ ?
    CLERK: Uh, it's $.55.
    CUSTOMER: And these _____ ?
    CLERK: They're $1.00.
    CUSTOMER: Thank you.

4. CUSTOMER: Excuse me. How much are these _____ ?
    CLERK: They're $.80.
    CUSTOMER: And this _____ ?
    CLERK: $.50.

FOLLOW UP

Exercise 5

Work with a partner.
Student A asks the price of an item or items.
Student B reads a price.
Student A circles the price.
Student B looks at the price. Is it the right one?

Now Student B asks the price of an item or items.
Student A reads a price.
Student B circles the price.

1. STUDENT A: How much is this envelope?

   $ .67   ($ .66) $1.66 $ .76

   STUDENT B: It's $ .66.

 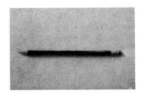

2. STUDENT B: How much are these envelopes?

   99¢   88¢   79¢   (98¢)

   STUDENT A: They're 98¢.

 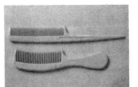

3. STUDENT A: .... ?

   $1.25 $1.35 $1.45 $1.55

   STUDENT B: ....

4. STUDENT B: . . . . ?

  18¢   80¢   19¢   90¢

STUDENT A: . . . .

5. STUDENT A: . . . . ?

  $4.07 $4.17 $4.70 $4.77

STUDENT B: . . . .

6. STUDENT B: . . . . ?

  $1.60 $1.16 $ .60 $ .16

STUDENT A: . . . .

Exercise 6

Write the name of the items in each picture.

1. batteries

2. _____

3. _____

4. _____

5. _____

6. _____

Mommy, what are you doing?

Look at the pictures and listen.

1.

2.

3.

4.

5.

6.

FOCUS

Exercise 1

Listen to the sentences. Match the sentences with the pictures.

_____

_1_

_____

_____

_____

Exercise 2

Number the sentences as you hear them.

_____ I'm making hamburgers.

_____ I'm making a phone call.

_____ I'm kissing Daddy.

___1___ What are you doing?

_____ I'm washing the dishes.

_____ I'm typing a letter.

_____ I'm taking a shower.

Exercise 3

Listen to the sounds and complete the sentences.

taking   making   dishes
washing   kissing   shower
typing   call   letter

1. I'm _making_ hamburgers.

2. I'm _____ a phone _____ .

3. I'm _____ Daddy.

4. I'm _____ a _____ .

5. I'm _____ the _____ .

6. I'm _____ a _____ .

FOLLOW UP

Exercise 4

Fill in the balloons.
Then work with a partner and practice the conversations.

1. What are you doing?

2. What are you doing?

3. What are you doing?

4. What are you doing?

5. What are you doing?

6. What are you doing?

I'm looking for a hat.

1.

Look at the pictures and listen.

2.

3.

4.

5.

6.

7.

8.

FOCUS

Exercise 1

Listen to the sentences and circle the matching pictures.

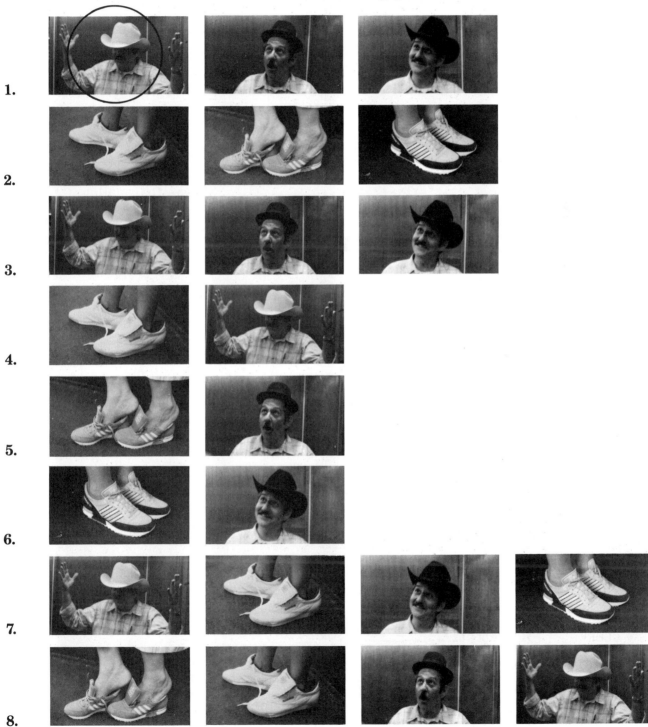

Exercise 2

Number the sentences as you hear them.

_____ It's too big.

_____ Yes, it's perfect.

_____ How about this one?

_____ Yes, I'm looking for a hat.

_____ What about this one?

_____ How about this?

_____ It's too small.

__1__ May I help you?

Exercise 3

Number the sentences as you hear them.

__1__ May I help you?

_____ What about these?

_____ Oh, they're too big.

_____ I'm looking for some shoes.

_____ How about these?

_____ Well, how about these?

_____ No, they're too small.

_____ Yes, they're fine.

Exercise 4

Complete the conversations.

hat	this	small
shoes	help	perfect
too		

1. CLERK: May I __help__ you?

   CUSTOMER: Yes, I'm looking for some _____ .

   CLERK: How about these?

   CUSTOMER: They're too _____ .

   CLERK: Or these?

   CUSTOMER: Yes, they're _____ .

2. CLERK: May I help you?

   CUSTOMER: Yes, I need a _____ .

   CLERK: How about _____ ?

   CUSTOMER: No, it's _____ big.

   CLERK: What about this one?

   CUSTOMER: Yes, it's fine.

FOLLOW UP

Exercise 5

Work with a partner.
Student A describes an item or items in the picture.
Student B circles the picture.
Student A looks at the picture. Is it the right one?

Now Student B describes an item or items in the picture.
Student A circles the picture.

1. STUDENT A SPEAKS: It's too small.
   STUDENT B WRITES.

2. STUDENT B SPEAKS: They're too big.
   STUDENT A WRITES.

 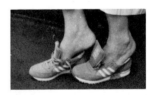 

3. STUDENT A: . . . .

4. STUDENT B: . . . .

5. STUDENT A: . . . .

6. STUDENT B: . . . .

 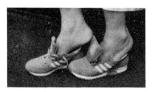

7. STUDENT A: . . . .

8. STUDENT B: . . . .

Look at the schedule and listen.

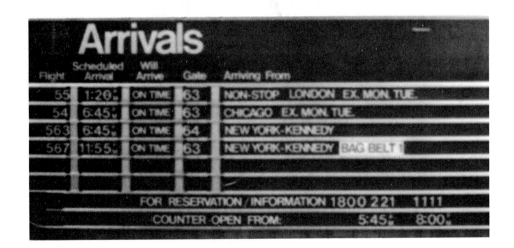

FOCUS

Exercise 1

Listen to the question, look at the schedule and write the answer.

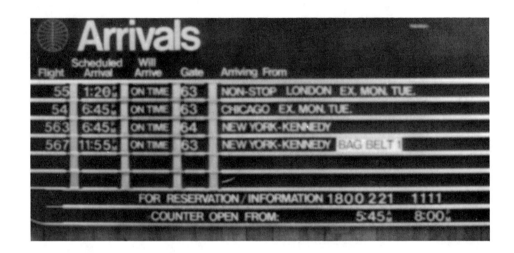

1. at 6:45 p.m.   6. _____

2. at Gate 63   7. _____

3. at 11:55 p.m.   8. _____

4. _____   9. _____

5. _____   10. _____

Exercise 2

Number the sentences as you hear them.

_____ At Gate 63.

__1__ What time does Flight 55 arrive?

_____ Thank you.

_____ Let's see. At 6:45 P.M., sir.

_____ At 1:20 P.M., ma'am.

_____ Thanks.

_____ When does Flight 563 arrive?

_____ Thanks a lot.

_____ Where does Flight 54 arrive?

Exercise 3

Complete the conversations.

When	Where	Thanks	a lot
What time	P.M.	Thank you	arrive

1. FIRST PERSON: Excuse me. _What time_ does Flight 563 arrive?

   AGENT: Flight 563? At 6:45 _____ .

   FIRST PERSON: OK. _____ .

2. SECOND PERSON: _____ does Flight 567 _____ ?

   AGENT: Flight 567? At Gate 63.

   SECOND PERSON: Thanks _____ .

3. THIRD PERSON: Excuse me. _____ does Flight 55 arrive?

   AGENT: Let's see. At 1:20 P.M.

   THIRD PERSON: _____ .

FOLLOW UP

Exercise 4

Work with a partner.
Student A asks five questions about the schedule (*What time. . .? When. . .? Where. . .?*).
Student B looks at the schedule and answers the questions. Are they the right answers?

Now Student B asks five questions about the schedule.
Student A looks at the schedule and answers.

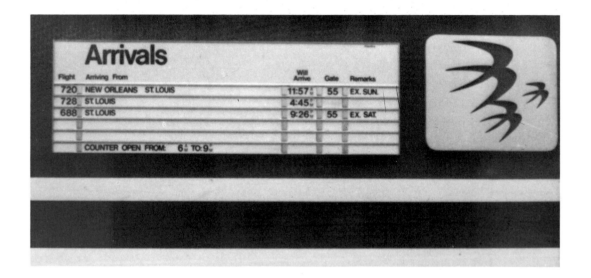

Flight	Arriving From	Will Arrive	Gate	Remarks
720	NEW ORLEANS ST. LOUIS	11:57	55	EX. SUN.
728	ST. LOUIS	4:45		
688	ST. LOUIS	9:26	55	EX. SAT.

COUNTER OPEN FROM: 6 TO 9

Where is the 51st Street station?

Look at the pictures and listen.

1.

2.

3.

4.

5.

6.

FOCUS

Exercise 1

Listen to the sentences. Match the sentences with the pictures.

_____

_____

_____

__1__

_____

Exercise 2

Put your finger at the bottom of the map (on START HERE). Follow the instructions. Then write your answers.

1. _at the bank_   4. _____

2. _____   5. _____

3. _____

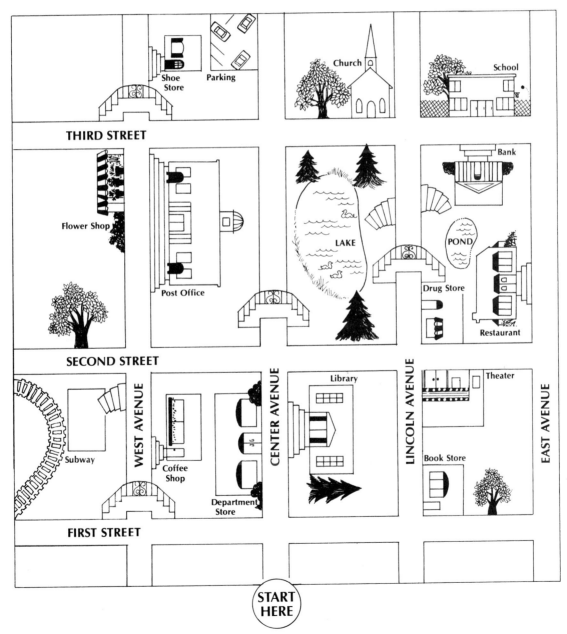

Exercise 3

Number the sentences as you hear them.

_____ Go under the bridge.

_____ Thank you very much.

_____ Then turn left at First Avenue.

___1___ Excuse me. Where is the 51st Street station?

_____ Go straight on 53rd Street.

_____ Go up the steps.

_____ And then turn right at 51st Street.

_____ Go down the steps and there's the station.

FOLLOW UP

Exercise 4

Work with a partner.
Look at the map on page 71.
Put your finger at the bottom of the page (on **START HERE**).
Student A gives directions to three places.
Student B writes the name of each place.
Student A looks at the names. Are they the right ones?

Now Student B gives directions to three places.
Student A writes the name of each place.

1. _____

2. _____

3. _____

Exercise 5

Complete the sentences.

steps
turn
down

right
under
straight

1. Turn **right**.

2. Go _____ the bridge.

3. Go _____ the steps.

4. Go _____.

5. Go up the _____.

6. _____ left.

TAPESCRIPT

UNIT 1

Ten singles, please.

NARRATOR: Look at the pictures and listen.
TELLER: Next!
CUSTOMER: Ten singles, please.
TELLER: OK. Ten dollars. One . . . Two . . . Three . . . Four . . . Five . . . Six . . . Seven . . . Eight . . . Nine . . . Ten.
CUSTOMER: Thanks.
NARRATOR: Now look at the pictures again and listen.

(Repetition of above)

Exercise 1
NARRATOR: Listen and circle the number you hear.

Five
Seven
Two
Nine
Eight
Four
Ten
Six

Exercise 2
NARRATOR: Listen and write the number you hear.

Eight singles, please.
Two dollars.
Five singles, please.
Three dollars.
Nine singles, please.
Seven dollars.
Ten singles, please.
One dollar.

Exercise 3
NARRATOR: Look at the words and listen.

One Two Three Four Five
Six Seven Eight Nine Ten

Exercise 4
NARRATOR: Listen and circle the word you hear.

Six
Three
Eight
Five
Seven
Two

UNIT 2

That's 626-2834.

NARRATOR: Look at the pictures and listen.

One.
OPERATOR: May I help you?
VOICE 1: Foo Chow restaurant, please.
OPERATOR: That's six two six, two eight three four.
VOICE 1: Thanks.
NARRATOR: Two.
OPERATOR: May I help you?
VOICE 2: Legal Aid, please.
OPERATOR: That's five seven seven, three three oh one.
VOICE 2: Thanks.
NARRATOR: Three.
OPERATOR: May I help you?
VOICE 3: Park Hospital, please.
OPERATOR: Eight two eight, seven eight eight seven.
VOICE 3: Excuse me?
OPERATOR: Eight two eight, seven eight eight seven.
VOICE 3: Thank you.
NARRATOR: Four.
OPERATOR: May I help you?
VOICE 4: Hotel George Washington, please.
OPERATOR: That's two five oh, four nine three two.
VOICE 4: Thanks.
NARRATOR: Five
OPERATOR: May I help you?
VOICE 5: TWA, please.
OPERATOR: That's six nine one, two three oh three.
VOICE 5: Please repeat that.
OPERATOR: Six nine one, two three oh three.

VOICE 5: Thank you.
NARRATOR: Six.
OPERATOR: May I help you?
VOICE 6: City Bank, please.
OPERATOR: Five eight seven, five one six oh.
VOICE 6: Thank you.
NARRATOR: Now look at the pictures again and listen.

(Repetition of above, minus narrator's voice)

Exercise 1

NARRATOR: Listen and circle the number you hear.

OPERATOR: Five three six, four two oh two.
OPERATOR: Three four five, nine seven five two.
OPERATOR: Four five four, eight nine seven six.
OPERATOR: Seven seven eight, two oh four six.
OPERATOR: Six two six, one one three nine.
OPERATOR: Two five five, seven five oh nine.
OPERATOR: Eight seven two, three three eight six.
OPERATOR: Eight seven one, oh four eight two.

Exercise 2

NARRATOR: Listen and write the missing numbers.

OPERATOR: May I help you?
CALLER 1: Memorial Hospital, please.
OPERATOR: That's five nine eight, three two five seven.
OPERATOR: May I help you?
CALLER 2: Holiday Hotel, please.
OPERATOR: Two eight nine, one five eight two.
CALLER 2: Thank you.
OPERATOR: May I help you?
CALLER 3: Lincoln Bank, please.
OPERATOR: Seven four two, six two nine four.
CALLER 3: Please repeat that.
OPERATOR: Seven four two, six two nine four.
CALLER 3: Thanks.
OPERATOR: May I help you?
CALLER 4: Paul's Restaurant, please.
OPERATOR: That's nine nine five, seven one six oh.
CALLER 4: Thank you.
OPERATOR: May I help you?
CALLER 5: Jackson Police, please.
OPERATOR: Three five seven, four oh two two.
OPERATOR: May I help you?
CALLER 6: Legal Aid, please.
OPERATOR: OK. Six five two, two seven two six.
CALLER 6: Excuse me?

OPERATOR: That's six five two, two seven two six.
CALLER 6: Thanks a lot.
OPERATOR: May I help you?
CALLER 7: Yes. Beach Cafe, please.
OPERATOR: That's four eight one, seven oh four five.
CALLER 7: Thank you.
OPERATOR: May I help you?
CALLER 8: City Health Center.
OPERATOR: Nine two one, five five three eight.

Exercise 3

NARRATOR: Listen and write the number you hear.

OPERATOR: Four six two, eight oh six nine.
OPERATOR: Three three two, five one seven eight.
OPERATOR: Six nine three, one five one eight.
OPERATOR: Eight five five, four eight oh four.
OPERATOR: Seven seven one, five one seven eight.
OPERATOR: Eight seven one, oh five oh seven.
OPERATOR: Five five six, two one oh five.
OPERATOR: Nine eight eight, two seven two oh.

UNIT 3
Change for a twenty, please.

NARRATOR: Look at the pictures and listen.
TELLER: Next, please!
CUSTOMER: Change for a twenty, please.
TELLER: OK. Ten . . . Eleven . . . Twelve . . . Thirteen . . . Fourteen . . . Fifteen . . . Sixteen . . . Seventeen . . . Eighteen . . . Nineteen . . . Twenty dollars.
CUSTOMER: Thank you.
NARRATOR: Now look at the pictures again and listen.

(Repetition of above)

Exercise 1

NARRATOR: Listen and circle the number you hear.

Twelve
Sixteen
Eighteen
Nineteen
Seventeen
Twenty
Fourteen
Eleven

Exercise 2

NARRATOR: Listen and write the number you hear.

Twelve dollars.
Fifteen singles, please.
Seventeen dollars.
Change for a twenty, please.
Eleven dollars.
Thirteen dollars.
Change for a ten, please.
Eighteen dollars.

Exercise 3

NARRATOR: Look at the words and listen.

Eleven Twelve Thirteen Fourteen Fifteen Sixteen Seventeen Eighteen Nineteen Twenty.

Exercise 4

NARRATOR: Listen and circle the word you hear.

Sixteen
Eleven
Seventeen
Twelve
Five
Nineteen

UNIT 4

Ten tens, please.

NARRATOR: Look at the pictures and listen.

TELLER: Next!
CUSTOMER: Ten tens, please.
TELLER: Sure. Ten . . . Twenty . . . Thirty . . . Forty . . . Fifty . . . Sixty . . . Seventy . . . Eighty . . . Ninety . . . One hundred dollars.
CUSTOMER: Thanks.

NARRATOR: Look at the pictures again and listen.

(*Repetition of above*)

Exercise 1

NARRATOR: Listen and circle the number you hear.

Thirty
Sixty
Fourteen
Ninety
Twenty

Eleven
Fifty
Seventeen

Exercise 2

NARRATOR: Listen and write the number you hear.

Seventy dollars, please.
Fifteen singles, please.
Change for a hundred, please.
Eighty dollars.
Forty singles, please.
Thirteen dollars.
Sixty singles, please.
Eleven dollars.

Exercise 3

NARRATOR: Look at the words and listen.

Ten Twenty Thirty Forty Fifty Sixty Seventy Eighty Ninety One hundred.

Exercise 4

NARRATOR: Listen and circle the word you hear.

Forty
Seventeen
Ninety
Twelve
Sixty
Thirty

UNIT 5

What's your address?

NARRATOR: Look at the pictures and listen.
One.
VOICE 1: City Health Center.
VOICE 2: Hello. What's your address?
VOICE 1: 25 Sutton Place South.
VOICE 2: Thank you.
NARRATOR: Two.
VOICE 3: Jane's Beauty Salon.
VOICE 4: Hi. What's your address?
VOICE 3: 75 Bleeker Street.
VOICE 4: Thanks.
NARRATOR: Three.
VOICE 5: Hoffman Employment Agency.
VOICE 6: Hello. Where are you located?
VOICE 5: At 230 Park Avenue.
VOICE 6: Excuse me?

VOICE 5:   230 Park.
VOICE 6:   Thank you.
NARRATOR: Four.
VOICE 7:   Shinbashi Restaurant.
VOICE 8:   What's your address?
VOICE 7:   200 Park Avenue.
VOICE 8:   OK. Thanks.
NARRATOR: Five.
VOICE 9:   Savings Bank.
VOICE 10:   Yes. Where are you located?
VOICE 9:   We're at 825 Third Avenue.
VOICE 10:   All right. Thanks.
NARRATOR: Six.
VOICE 11:   Passport Office.
VOICE 12:   What's your address?
VOICE 11:   410 East 57th Street.
VOICE 12:   Thank you.
NARRATOR: Seven.
VOICE 13:   Border's Books.
VOICE 14:   Where are you located?
VOICE 13:   We're at 1184 No. Main Street.
VOICE 14:   1184 No. Main Street?
VOICE 13:   That's right.
VOICE 14:   OK. Thank you very much.
NARRATOR: Eight.
VOICE 15:   North General Hospital.
VOICE 16:   What's your address?
VOICE 15:   1919 Church Street.
VOICE 16:   Thanks.
NARRATOR: Now look at the pictures again and listen.

(*Repetition of above, minus narrator's voice*)

Exercise 1

NARRATOR: Listen and circle the address you hear.
            One.
VOICE 1:   Six sixty-five State Street.
NARRATOR: Two.
VOICE 2:   Eighty-three East Avenue.
NARRATOR: Three.
VOICE 3:   Four twenty-eight Pine Street.
NARRATOR: Four.
VOICE 4:   Fourteen oh four Spring Road.
NARRATOR: Five.
VOICE 5:   One twenty-nine Lake Avenue.
NARRATOR: Six.
VOICE 6:   Fifty-two oh six Main Street.
NARRATOR: Seven.
VOICE 7:   Fifty-seven ninety Elm Street.
NARRATOR: Eight.
VOICE 8:   Four thirty-four Lincoln Avenue.

Exercise 2

NARRATOR: Listen and write the missing numbers.
            One.
VOICE 1:   Three twenty-five South Street.
NARRATOR: Two.
VOICE 2:   Twelve fifty-four Brook Avenue.
NARRATOR: Three.
VOICE 3:   Three eleven Bay Road.
NARRATOR: Four.
VOICE 4:   Fifteen sixty-eight Grand Avenue.
NARRATOR: Five.
VOICE 5:   Seventy-six oh four First Street.
NARRATOR: Six.
VOICE 6:   Five ninety-eight River Road.
NARRATOR: Seven.
VOICE 7:   Ten ninety-two Madison Avenue.
NARRATOR: Eight.
VOICE 8:   Two oh two Mountain Lane.

Exercise 3

NARRATOR: Listen and write the address you hear.
            One.
VOICE 1:   Tom's Restaurant.
VOICE 2:   What's your address, please?
VOICE 1:   Seven forty-two Main Street.
VOICE 2:   Thanks.
NARRATOR: Two.
VOICE 3:   City Bank.
VOICE 4:   What's your address, please?
VOICE 3:   Thirteen oh eight Linden Avenue.
VOICE 4:   Thank you.
NARRATOR: Three.
VOICE 5:   Century Cinema.
VOICE 6:   Where are you located?
VOICE 5:   We're at six twenty-five Church Road.
VOICE 6:   Excuse me?
VOICE 5:   Six twenty-five Church Road.
VOICE 6:   OK. Thanks.
NARRATOR: Four.
VOICE 7:   Crown Book Store.
VOICE 8:   What's your address?
VOICE 7:   Four twenty Oak Street.
VOICE 8:   Thank you.
NARRATOR: Five.
VOICE 9:   Public Library.
VOICE 10:   Where are you located?
VOICE 9:   Seventy-five thirty Penfield Road.
VOICE 10:   Seventy-five thirty?
VOICE 9:   Yes. Penfield Road.
VOICE 10:   Thanks a lot.
NARRATOR: Six.

VOICE 11: Betty's Boutique.
VOICE 12: What's your address?
VOICE 11: Fifty-three Lake Avenue.
VOICE 12: Thank you.

UNIT 6

Your name, please.

NARRATOR: Look at the pictures and listen.
One.
NAMETAKER: Your name, please.
ADULT 1: Mr. Dinn. D-i-n-n.
NAMETAKER: Uh-huh.
NARRATOR: Two.
NAMETAKER: Name, please.
Adult 2: Mrs. Rindell. R-i-n-d-e-l-l.
NARRATOR: Three.
NAMETAKER: Your name, sir.
Adult 3: Reid. R-e-i-d.
NAMETAKER: OK.
NARRATOR: Four.
NAMETAKER: Next.
ADULT 4: Soleri. S-o-l-e-r-i.
NAMETAKER: Umm-hum.
NARRATOR: Five.
NAMETAKER: Your name, ma'am.
ADULT 5: Mrs. Flores. F-l-o-r-e-s.
NAMETAKER: Excuse me?
ADULT 5: F-l-o-r-e-s.
NARRATOR: Six.
NAMETAKER: Yes. . .Next.
ADULT 6: Toledo. T-o-l-e-d-o.
NAMETAKER: OK.
NARRATOR: Seven.
NAMETAKER: Sir?
ADULT 7: Mr. Westoff. W-e-s-t-o-f-f.
NARRATOR: Eight.
NAMETAKER: Your name, miss.
ADULT 8: Ferrings. F-e-r-r-i-n-g-s.
NARRATOR: Nine.
NAMETAKER: Next. Sir?
ADULT 9: Konikow. K-o-n-i-k-o-w.
NAMETAKER: Uh-huh.
NARRATOR: Ten.
NAMETAKER: Ma'am?
ADULT 10: Mrs. Krieger. K-r-i-e-g-e-r.
NAMETAKER: Please repeat that.
ADULT 10: K-r-i-e-g-e-r.
NARRATOR: Now look at the pictures again and listen.

(*Repetition of above, minus narrator's voice*)

Exercise 1

NARRATOR: **Listen and write the missing letter.**
One.
VOICE 1: D-w-i-r-e.
NARRATOR: Two.
VOICE 2: R-o-d-i-n.
NARRATOR: Three.
VOICE 3: N-e-l-s-o-n.
NARRATOR: Four.
VOICE 4: G-o-r-d-o-n.
NARRATOR: Five.
VOICE 5: F-e-n-g.
NARRATOR: Six.
VOICE 6: W-e-i-l.
NARRATOR: Seven.
VOICE 7: K-i-t-t-s.
NARRATOR: Eight.
VOICE 8: S-i-n-g-e-r.
NARRATOR: Nine.
VOICE 9: L-a-n-g.
NARRATOR: Ten.
VOICE 10: F-o-s-t-e-r.

Exercise 2

NARRATOR: **Listen and circle the name you hear.**
One.
NAMETAKER: Your name, please.
VOICE 1: Dine. D-i-n-e.
NARRATOR: Two.
NAMETAKER: OK. Name, please.
VOICE 2: Fenn. F-e-n-n.
NAMETAKER: Excuse me?
VOICE 2: F-e-n-n.
NARRATOR: Three.
NAMETAKER: Next.
VOICE 3: Mr. Gent. G-e-n-t.
NARRATOR: Four.
NAMETAKER: Your name, sir
VOICE 4: Leff. L-e-f-f.
NAMETAKER: Uh-huh.
NARRATOR: Five.
NAMETAKER: Ma'am?
VOICE 5: Mrs. Keen. K-e-e-n.
NARRATOR: Six.
NAMETAKER: Your name?
VOICE 6: Teng. T-e-n-g.
NAMETAKER: Repeat that please.
VOICE 6: T-e-n-g.
NARRATOR: Seven.
NAMETAKER: Uh, your name, please.
VOICE 7: F-i-n-n.

NARRATOR: Eight.
NAMETAKER: OK. Next. Your name?
VOICE 8:   Stolt. S-t-o-l-t.

Exercise 3

NARRATOR: Listen and write the missing letter.
              One.
VOICE 1:   L-e-o-n.
NARRATOR: Two.
VOICE 2:   D-r-e-w.
NARRATOR: Three.
VOICE 3:   F-i-d-l-e-r.
NARRATOR: Four.
VOICE 4:   K-e-l-l-e-r.
NARRATOR: Five.
VOICE 5:   D-o-d-g-e.
NARRATOR: Six.
VOICE 6:   E-t-o-n.
NARRATOR: Seven.
VOICE 7:   G-i-l-l.
NARRATOR: Eight.
VOICE 8:   F-e-l-d.
NARRATOR: Nine.
VOICE 9:   R-o-t-k-i-n.
NARRATOR: Ten.
VOICE 10:   T-i-l-s-o-n.

Exercise 4

NARRATOR: Listen and write the names.
              One.
VOICE 1:   F-o-r-d.
NARRATOR: Two.
VOICE 2:   L-o-w.
NARRATOR: Three.
VOICE 3:   K-i-n-g.
NARRATOR: Four.
VOICE 4:   G-o-r-e.
NARRATOR: Five.
VOICE 5:   N-i-l-e-s.
NARRATOR: Six.
VOICE 6:   S-o-l-d-o.
NARRATOR: Seven.
VOICE 7:   S-n-e-e-d.
NARRATOR: Eight.
VOICE 8:   T-e-w-e-l.
NARRATOR: Nine.
VOICE 9:   L-i-e-f.
NARRATOR: Ten.
VOICE 10:   D-e-n-e-s.

UNIT 7

Spell it, please.

NARRATOR: Look at the pictures and listen.
              One.
NAMETAKER: Spell it, please.
ADULT 1:   C-h-a-n.
NAMETAKER: OK.
NARRATOR: Two.
NAMETAKER: And your name?
ADULT 2:   Zachary. Z-a-c-h-a-r-y.
NAMETAKER: Excuse me?
ADULT 2:   Z-a-c-h-a-r-y.
NARRATOR: Three.
NAMETAKER: Next. Ma'am?
ADULT 3:   Mrs. Jacoby. J-a-c-o-b-y.
NARRATOR: Four.
NAMETAKER: Next.
ADULT 4:   Mr. Zimmer. Z-i-m-m-e-r.
NAMETAKER: Uh-huh.
NARRATOR: Five.
NAMETAKER: Sir?
ADULT 5:   Buxton. B-u-x-t-o-n.
NAMETAKER: OK.
NARRATOR: Six.
NAMETAKER: Your name, miss.
ADULT 6:   Ms. Ajax. A-j-a-x.
NAMETAKER: Mmm-hum.
NARRATOR: Seven.
NAMETAKER: Next.
ADULT 7:   Quincy. Q-u-i-n-c-y.
NARRATOR: Eight.
NAMETAKER: Yes. . .Sir?
ADULT 8:   Mr. Paquette. P-a-q-u-e-t-t-e.
NARRATOR: Nine.
NAMETAKER: Ma'am?
ADULT 9:   Mrs. Mavis. M-a-v-i-s.
NAMETAKER: Please repeat that.
ADULT 9:   M-a-v-i-s.
NAMETAKER: OK.
NARRATOR: Ten.
NAMETAKER: Your name?
ADULT 10:   Pavlov.
NAMETAKER: Spell it, please.
ADULT 10:   P-a-v-l-o-v.
NARRATOR: Now look at the pictures again and
              listen.

(*Repetition of above, minus narrator's voice*)

Exercise 1

NARRATOR: Listen and write the missing letter.
              One.

VOICE 1:   B-e-a-n-e.
NARRATOR: Two.
VOICE 2:   M-u-l-l-e-r.
NARRATOR: Three.
VOICE 3:   Z-h-a-n-g.
NARRATOR: Four.
VOICE 4:   C-o-w-e-n.
NARRATOR: Five.
VOICE 5:   V-o-s-s.
NARRATOR: Six.
VOICE 6:   M-o-x-e-y.
NARRATOR: Seven.
VOICE 7:   G-i-l-e-s.
NARRATOR: Eight.
VOICE 8:   B-y-e-r.
NARRATOR: Nine.
VOICE 9:   L-e-v-y.
NARRATOR: Ten.
VOICE 10: H-a-i-l-e.

Exercise 2

NARRATOR: Listen and circle the name you hear.
            One.
VOICE 1:   Bacher.
NAMETAKER: Spell it, please.
VOICE 1:   B-a-c-h-e-r.
NARRATOR: Two.
NAMETAKER: Your name, miss.
VOICE 2:   Feliz. F-e-l-i-z.
NARRATOR: Three.
NAMETAKER: Next.
VOICE 3:   Kohan. K-o-h-a-n.
NAMETAKER: Repeat that please.
VOICE 3:   K-o-h-a-n.
NARRATOR: Four.
NAMETAKER: Your name, sir.
VOICE 4:   Chan. C-h-a-n.
NARRATOR: Five.
NAMETAKER: Ma'am?
VOICE 5:   Mrs. Barker. B-a-r-k-e-r.
NARRATOR: Six.
NAMETAKER: Next.
VOICE 6:   Moar. M-o-a-r.
NAMETAKER: Excuse me?
VOICE 6:   M-o-a-r.
NAMETAKER: OK.
NARRATOR: Seven.
NAMETAKER: Your name?
VOICE 7:   Gant. G-a-n-t.

NARRATOR: Eight.
NAMETAKER: Miss?
VOICE 8:   Major. M-a-j-o-r.

Exercise 3

NARRATOR: Listen and write the missing letter.
          One.
VOICE 1:   S-h-a-r-p.
NARRATOR: Two.
VOICE 2:   U-n-g-e-r.
NARRATOR: Three.
VOICE 3:   R-y-a-n.
NARRATOR: Four.
VOICE 4:   M-u-r-p-h-y.
NARRATOR: Five.
VOICE 5:   D-i-x-o-n.
NARRATOR: Six.
VOICE 6:   S-t-a-h-l.
NARRATOR: Seven.
VOICE 7:   D-e-v-l-i-n.
NARRATOR: Eight.
VOICE 8:   N-a-g-l-e-r.
NARRATOR: Nine.
VOICE 9 :   W-i-n-e-r.
NARRATOR: Ten.
VOICE 10: A-r-i-z-a.

Exercise 4

NARRATOR: Listen and write the names.
          One.
VOICE 1:   J-a-m-e-s.
NARRATOR: Two.
VOICE 2:   R-u-b-i-n.
NARRATOR: Three.
VOICE 3:   P-a-i-n-e.
NARRATOR: Four.
VOICE 4:   Q-u-i-n-n.
NARRATOR: Five.
VOICE 5:   M-y-l-e-s.
NARRATOR: Six.
VOICE 6:   F-i-x-x.
NARRATOR: Seven.
VOICE 7:   J-o-y-c-e.
NARRATOR: Eight.
VOICE 8:   B-r-o-w-n.
NARRATOR: Nine.
VOICE 9:   V-e-l-e-z.
NARRATOR: Ten.
VOICE 10: Y-o-r-k.

UNIT 8

What would you like to eat?

NARRATOR: Look at the pictures and listen.
MOTHER: What would you like to eat?
NARRATOR: One.
MOTHER: Chicken?
CHILD: Uhhhhh.........
NARRATOR: Two.
MOTHER: Fish?
CHILD: Ummm......
NARRATOR: Three.
MOTHER: A steak?
NARRATOR: Four.
MOTHER: How about a hamburger?
CHILD: Mmmmm....
NARRATOR: Five.
MOTHER: A hot dog?
CHILD: Uh-uh.
NARRATOR: Six.
MOTHER: French fries?
CHILD: Noooo....
NARRATOR: Seven.
MOTHER: Salad?
NARRATOR: Eight.
MOTHER: A sandwich?
CHILD: A sandwich. Yes! I'd like a sandwich.
MOTHER: OK. What would you like to drink?
NARRATOR: Nine.
MOTHER: Milk?
CHILD: Ummmm.....
NARRATOR: Ten.
MOTHER: A Coke?
NARRATOR: Eleven.
MOTHER: Water?
CHILD: Uh-uh.
NARRATOR: Twelve.
MOTHER: A milkshake?
CHILD: A milkshake. Yes! I'd like a milkshake.
NARRATOR: Look at the pictures again and listen.

(*Repetition of above, minus narrator's voice*)

Exercise 1

NARRATOR: Listen to the questions. Match the questions with the pictures.
One.
MOTHER: A salad?
NARRATOR: Two.
MOTHER: Fish?
NARRATOR: Three.
MOTHER: French fries?
NARRATOR: Four.
MOTHER: A sandwich?
NARRATOR: Five.
MOTHER: A Coke?
NARRATOR: Six.
MOTHER: A hot dog?

Exercise 2

NARRATOR: Listen to the questions. Match the questions with the pictures.
One.
MOTHER: A steak?
NARRATOR: Two.
MOTHER: Milk?
NARRATOR: Three.
MOTHER: Water?
NARRATOR: Four.
MOTHER: A hamburger?
NARRATOR: Five.
MOTHER: A milkshake?
NARRATOR: Six.
MOTHER: Chicken?

Exercise 3

NARRATOR: Listen to the customers. Circle the food they order.
One.
WAITRESS: What would you like?
WOMAN: I'd like a steak, french fries, and coffee, please.
NARRATOR: Two.
WAITRESS: And what would you like?
MAN: Uh, a hamburger, please. And a salad.
WAITRESS: Anything to drink?
MAN: A Coke, please.
NARRATOR: Three.
WAITRESS: What would you like, sir?
MAN: Uh, I'd like chicken, a salad, and tea.
NARRATOR: Four.
WAITRESS: Ma'am?
WOMAN: Uh. . . .I'd like fish. . .and uh. . .french fries.
WAITRESS: And to drink?
WOMAN: Coffee, please.

Exercise 4

NARRATOR: Number the questions as you hear them.
One.
MOTHER: Fish?
NARRATOR: Two.

MOTHER: Coke?
NARRATOR: Three.
MOTHER: Water?
NARRATOR: Four.
MOTHER: Chicken?
NARRATOR: Five.
MOTHER: Milk?
NARRATOR: Six.
MOTHER: A hot dog?
NARRATOR: Seven.
MOTHER: A sandwich?
NARRATOR: Eight.
MOTHER: French fries?
NARRATOR: Nine.
MOTHER: A hamburger?
NARRATOR: Ten.
MOTHER: A milkshake?
NARRATOR: Eleven.
MOTHER: A salad?
NARRATOR: Twelve.
MOTHER: A steak?

Exercise 5

NARRATOR: Complete the conversations.
One.
WAITER: What would you like to eat?
WOMAN: I'd like a chicken sandwich, a salad and a Coke, please.
NARRATOR: Two.
WAITER: OK. And what would you like?
CHILD: I'd like a hot dog and french fries.
WAITER: And to drink?
CHILD: Milk, please.
NARRATOR: Three.
WAITER: Sir?
MAN: Um..the fish, please.
WAITER: Anything to drink?
MAN: Coffee. . .and some water.
NARRATOR: Four.
WAITER: OK. What would you like, ma'am?
WOMAN: Chicken and french fries, please. And tea.

UNIT 9

Tell us about the apartment.

NARRATOR: Look at the pictures and listen.
HUSBAND: Tell us about the apartment.
NARRATOR: One.
AGENT: Well. . .There's a living room.

NARRATOR: Two.
AGENT: There's a kitchen. . .
NARRATOR: Three.
AGENT: A dining room. . . .
NARRATOR: Four.
AGENT: Uh. . . .and one bathroom.
NARRATOR: Five.
AGENT: There's one bedroom.
NARRATOR: Six.
AGENT: Oh! And there's a balcony.
NARRATOR: Seven.
WIFE: Is there a fireplace?
AGENT: Um. . .no, there isn't a fireplace.
NARRATOR: Eight.
WIFE: Is there a garage?
AGENT: No, there isn't.
NARRATOR: Now look at the pictures again and listen.

(*Repetition of above, minus narrator's voice*)

Exercise 1

NARRATOR: Listen to the sentences. Match the sentences with the pictures.
One.
AGENT: There's one bedroom.
NARRATOR: Two.
AGENT: And one bathroom.
NARRATOR: Three.
AGENT: There's a kitchen.
NARRATOR: Four.
AGENT: There's a living room.
NARRATOR: Five.
AGENT: And there's a dining room.
NARRATOR: Six.
AGENT: But there isn't a fireplace.
NARRATOR: Seven.
AGENT: And. . .um. . .there isn't a garage.
NARRATOR: Eight.
AGENT: But there is a balcony.

Exercise 2

NARRATOR: Listen to the conversation. Does the apartment have the item in the picture? Circle *yes* or *no*.
WIFE: Tell us about the apartment.
NARRATOR: One.
AGENT: Well, there's a living room.
NARRATOR: Two.
AGENT: There isn't a dining room.
NARRATOR: Three.
AGENT: Uh, there's one bedroom.

NARRATOR: Four.
HUSBAND: Is there a balcony?
AGENT: Uh, no. There isn't a balcony.
NARRATOR: Five.
AGENT: There's one bathroom.
NARRATOR: Six.
AGENT: And a kitchen.
NARRATOR: Seven.
AGENT: Uh . . . there isn't a garage.
NARRATOR: Eight.
WIFE: Is there a fireplace?
AGENT: Oh, yes, there is.

Exercise 3

NARRATOR: Number the sentences as you hear them.
HUSBAND: Tell us about the apartment.
AGENT: Well. . .There's a living room. . .There's a kitchen. . .A dining room. . . Uh. . .and one bathroom. . .There's one bedroom. . .Oh! And there's a balcony.
WIFE: Is there a fireplace?
AGENT: Um. . .no, there isn't a fireplace.
WIFE: Is there a garage?
AGENT: No, there isn't.

UNIT 10

I need your name.

NARRATOR: Look at the pictures and listen.
One.
REGISTRAR: I need your name.
STUDENT: OK.
NARRATOR: Two.
REGISTRAR: Your address.
STUDENT: Uh-huh.
NARRATOR: Three.
REGISTRAR: Your phone number.
NARRATOR: Four.
REGISTRAR: And your signature.
NARRATOR: Five.
REGISTRAR: I need a check for five dollars.
STUDENT: OK.
NARRATOR: Six.
REGISTRAR: And a photograph.
STUDENT: Here.
NARRATOR: Now look at the pictures again and listen.

(Repetition of above, minus narrator's voice)

Exercise 1

NARRATOR: Circle the item you hear.
One.
VOICE 1: I need a photograph.
NARRATOR: Two.
VOICE 2: I need your signature.
NARRATOR: Three.
VOICE 3: I need your phone number.
NARRATOR: Four.
VOICE 4: I need a check for five dollars.
NARRATOR: Five.
VOICE 5: I need your name and address.
NARRATOR: Six.
VOICE 6: I need a check for twenty dollars and a photograph.
NARRATOR: Seven.
VOICE 7: I need your signature and a photograph.
NARRATOR: Eight.
VOICE 8: I need your check, your address and your phone number.

Exercise 2

NARRATOR: Number the sentences as you hear them.
REGISTRAR: I need your address.
STUDENT: OK.
REGISTRAR: And your name and phone number.
REGISTRAR: I need a check for fifty dollars.
STUDENT: Here.
REGISTRAR: Your signature. . . .and a photograph. Thank you.

Exercise 3

NARRATOR: Listen and circle the sentence you hear.
One.
VOICE 1: I need a check for five dollars and a photograph.
NARRATOR: Two.
VOICE 2: I need a photograph and your address.
NARRATOR: Three.
VOICE 3: I need your name and signature.
NARRATOR: Four.
VOICE 4: I need your phone number and a check for fifteen dollars.
NARRATOR: Five.
VOICE 5: I need your signature and your check.
NARRATOR: Six.
VOICE 6: I need a check for thirty-five dollars, and your name and address.

UNIT 11

How much is this shampoo?

NARRATOR: Look at the pictures and listen.

One.

CUSTOMER: Excuse me. How much is this shampoo?

CLERK: It's a dollar seventy-nine.

NARRATOR: Two.

CUSTOMER: And how much is this toothpaste?

CLERK: It's a dollar twenty-five.

NARRATOR: Three.

CUSTOMER: And this aspirin?

CLERK: Two twenty-five.

NARRATOR: Four.

CUSTOMER: Excuse me. How much is this film?

CLERK: It's three oh nine.

NARRATOR: Five.

CUSTOMER: And how much is this cologne?

CLERK: It's five sixty.

NARRATOR: Six.

CUSTOMER: And this soap?

CLERK: A dollar thirty.

NARRATOR: Now look at the pictures again and listen.

(*Repetition of above, minus narrator's voice*)

Exercise 1

NARRATOR: Circle the item and the price you hear.

One.

CUSTOMER: How much is this aspirin?

CLERK: It's a dollar thirty-five.

NARRATOR: Two.

CUSTOMER: How much is this soap?

CLERK: It's a dollar seven.

NARRATOR: Three.

CUSTOMER: Excuse me. How much is this film?

CLERK: It's three thirty-nine.

NARRATOR: Four.

CUSTOMER: How much is this toothpaste?

CLERK: It's two oh five.

NARRATOR: Five.

CUSTOMER: How much is this shampoo?

CLERK: It's a dollar forty-nine.

NARRATOR: Six.

CUSTOMER: Excuse me. How much is this aspirin?

CLERK: It's two twenty.

Exercise 2

NARRATOR: Number the sentences as you hear them.

VOICE 1: How much is this film?

VOICE 2: How much is this shampoo?

VOICE 3: How much is this aspirin?

VOICE 4: How much is this soap?

VOICE 5: How much is this toothpaste?

VOICE 6: How much is this cologne?

Exercise 3

NARRATOR: Listen and write the missing number.

One.

CUSTOMER: How much is this soap?

CLERK: It's a dollar five.

NARRATOR: Two.

CUSTOMER: How much is this aspirin?

CLERK: It's four eighty-seven.

NARRATOR: Three.

CUSTOMER: How much is this film?

CLERK: It's four oh five.

NARRATOR: Four.

CUSTOMER: Excuse me. How much is this shampoo?

CLERK: It's two ninety-nine.

NARRATOR: Five.

CUSTOMER: How much is this cologne?

CLERK: It's three oh eight.

NARRATOR: Six.

CUSTOMER: Excuse me. How much is this toothpaste?

CLERK: It's two sixteen.

NARRATOR: Seven.

CUSTOMER: How much is this soap?

CLERK: It's a dollar twenty-seven.

NARRATOR: Eight.

CUSTOMER: How much is this aspirin?

CLERK: It's two fifty.

Exercise 4

NARRATOR: Listen and write the price you hear.

One.

CLERK: It's a dollar sixty.

NARRATOR: Two.

CLERK: It's two oh eight.

NARRATOR: Three.

CLERK: It's four fifteen.

NARRATOR: Four.

CLERK: It's three thirty-two.

NARRATOR: Five.

CLERK: It's a dollar seventy.

NARRATOR: Six.
CLERK: It's three seventy-nine.
NARRATOR: Seven.
CLERK: It's four oh five.
NARRATOR: Eight.
CLERK: It's a dollar eighty.
NARRATOR: Nine.
CLERK: It's two nineteen.
NARRATOR: Ten.
CLERK: It's four ninety-nine.

UNIT 12

How much are these vitamins?

NARRATOR: Look at the pictures and listen.
One.
CUSTOMER: Pardon me. How much are these vitamins?
CLERK: They're four fifty-five.
NARRATOR: Two.
CUSTOMER: And how much are these razors?
CLERK: They're eighty-five cents.
NARRATOR: Three.
CUSTOMER: And these combs?
CLERK: They're ninety-eight cents.
NARRATOR: Four.
CUSTOMER: Excuse me. How much are these envelopes?
CLERK: They're sixty-seven cents.
NARRATOR: Five.
CUSTOMER: And how much are these pencils?
CLERK: They're seventy-nine cents.
NARRATOR: Six.
CUSTOMER: And these batteries?
CLERK: A dollar nineteen.
NARRATOR: Now look at the pictures again and listen.

(*Repetition of above, minus narrator's voice*)

Exercise 1

NARRATOR: Circle the item and the price you hear.
One.
CUSTOMER: How much are these razors?
CLERK: They're ninety-eight cents.
NARRATOR: Two.
CUSTOMER: Excuse me. How much are these envelopes?

CLERK: They're seventy cents.
NARRATOR: Three.
CUSTOMER: How much are these pencils?
CLERK: They're a dollar eight.
NARRATOR: Four.
CUSTOMER: How much are these batteries?
CLERK: Uh, they're fifty cents.
NARRATOR: Five.
CUSTOMER: Excuse me. How much are these vitamins?
CLERK: Mmmm, four eighty-nine.
NARRATOR: Six.
CUSTOMER: How much are these combs?
CLERK: They're ninety-eight cents.

Exercise 2

NARRATOR: Listen and circle the item or items in each conversation.
One.
CUSTOMER: How much is this comb?
CLERK: Fifty cents.
NARRATOR: Two.
CUSTOMER: Excuse me. How much is this envelope?
CLERK: Uh, it's fifteen cents.
NARRATOR: Three.
CUSTOMER: And these batteries?
CLERK: Ninety-five cents.
NARRATOR: Four.
CUSTOMER: Excuse me. How much is this pencil?
CLERK: Five cents.
NARRATOR: Five.
CUSTOMER: And these razors?
CLERK: They're seventy-five cents.
NARRATOR: Six.
CUSTOMER: How much is this battery?
CLERK: Fifty cents.
NARRATOR: Seven.
CUSTOMER: And this comb?
CLERK: It's a dollar.
NARRATOR: Eight.
CUSTOMER: Excuse me. How much are these razors?
CLERK: Seventy-five cents.
NARRATOR: Nine.
CUSTOMER: How much are these pencils?
CLERK: They're fifteen cents.
NARRATOR: Ten.
CUSTOMER: And these envelopes?
CLERK: They're thirty cents.

Exercise 3

NARRATOR: Number the sentences as you hear them.

CUSTOMER: How much are these envelopes?

CLERK: They're two dollars.

CUSTOMER: How much is this battery?

CLERK: It's fifty cents.

CUSTOMER: How much are these batteries?

CLERK: They're a dollar.

CUSTOMER: How much is this comb?

CLERK: It's a dollar.

Exercise 4

NARRATOR: Complete the conversations. One.

CUSTOMER: Pardon me. How much are these vitamins?

CLERK: They're three dollars.

CUSTOMER: And how much is this razor?

CLERK: It's seventy-five cents.

CUSTOMER: Thanks.

NARRATOR: Two.

CUSTOMER: Excuse me. How much is this toothpaste?

CLERK: It's a dollar thirty.

CUSTOMER: And these razors?

CLERK: A dollar fifty.

NARRATOR: Three.

CUSTOMER: How much is this soap?

CLERK: Uh, it's fifty-five cents.

CUSTOMER: And these combs?

CLERK: They're a dollar.

CUSTOMER: Thank you.

NARRATOR: Four.

CUSTOMER: Excuse me. How much are these batteries?

CLERK: They're eighty cents.

CUSTOMER: And this comb?

CLERK: Fifty cents.

UNIT 13

Mommy, what are you doing?

NARRATOR: Look at the pictures and listen. One.

CHILD: Mommy, what are you doing?

MOTHER: I'm taking a shower.

NARRATOR: Two.

CHILD: Mommy, what are you doing?

MOTHER: I'm washing the dishes.

NARRATOR: Three.

CHILD: Mommy, now what are you doing?

MOTHER: I'm making a phone call.

NARRATOR: Four.

CHILD: Mommy, what are you doing?

MOTHER: I'm typing a letter.

NARRATOR: Five.

CHILD: Mommy, what are you doing?

MOTHER: I'm making hamburgers.

NARRATOR: Six.

CHILD: Mommy, now what are you doing?

MOTHER: I'm kissing Daddy!

NARRATOR: Now look at the pictures again and listen.

(*Repetition of above, minus narrator's voice*)

Exercise 1

NARRATOR: Listen to the sentences. Match the sentences with the pictures. One.

CHILD: Mommy, what are you doing?

MOTHER: I'm typing a letter.

NARRATOR: Two.

CHILD: Mommy, what are you doing?

MOTHER: I'm kissing Daddy.

NARRATOR: Three.

CHILD: Mommy, what are you doing?

MOTHER: I'm making hamburgers.

NARRATOR: Four.

CHILD: Mommy, what are you doing?

MOTHER: I'm taking a shower.

NARRATOR: Five.

CHILD: Mommy, what are you doing?

MOTHER: I'm washing the dishes.

NARRATOR: Six.

CHILD: Mommy, what are you doing?

MOTHER: I'm making a phone call.

Exercise 2

NARRATOR: Number the sentences as you hear them.

CHILD: What are you doing?

MOTHER: I'm typing a letter. . . . I'm making a phone call . . . I'm making hamburgers . . . I'm kissing Daddy . . . I'm washing the dishes . . . I'm taking a shower.

Exercise 3

NARRATOR: Listen to the sounds and complete the sentences. One.

Sound of frying.

NARRATOR: Two.
Sound   of phone dialing.
NARRATOR: Three.
Sound   of kissing.
NARRATOR: Four.
Sound   of typing.
NARRATOR: Five.
Sound   of doing dishes.
NARRATOR: Six.
Sound   of a shower.

UNIT 14

I'm looking for a hat.

NARRATOR: Look at the pictures and listen.
    One.
CLERK: May I help you?
CUSTOMER: I'm looking for a hat.
NARRATOR: Two.
CLERK: How about this one?
CUSTOMER: It's too big.
NARRATOR: Three.
CLERK: Um, how about this?
CUSTOMER: It's too small.
NARRATOR: Four.
CLERK: What about this one?
CUSTOMER: Yes, it's perfect!
NARRATOR: Five.
CLERK: May I help you?
CUSTOMER: Um. . .I'm looking for some shoes.
NARRATOR: Six.
CLERK: How about these?
CUSTOMER: Oh, they're too big.
NARRATOR: Seven.
CLERK: Well, how about these?
CUSTOMER: No. . .they're too small.
NARRATOR: Eight.
CLERK: What about these?
CUSTOMER: Yes, they're fine!
NARRATOR: Now look at the pictures again and listen.

(*Repetition of above, minus narrator's voice*)

Exercise 1
NARRATOR 1: Listen to the sentences and circle the matching pictures.
    One.
NARRATOR 2: It's too big.
NARRATOR 1: Two.
NARRATOR 2: They're too small.

NARRATOR 1: Three.
NARRATOR 2: It's perfect.
NARRATOR 1: Four.
NARRATOR 2: It's too big.
NARRATOR 1: Five.
NARRATOR 2: They're too small.
NARRATOR 1: Six.
NARRATOR 2: It's fine.
NARRATOR 1: Seven.
NARRATOR 2: They're fine.
NARRATOR 1: Eight.
NARRATOR 2: They're too small.

Exercise 2
NARRATOR: Number the sentences as you hear them.
CLERK: May I help you?
CUSTOMER: Yes, I'm looking for a hat.
CLERK: How about this one?
CUSTOMER: It's too big.
CLERK: Um, how about this?
CUSTOMER: It's too small.
CLERK: What about this one?
CUSTOMER: Yes, it's perfect!

Exercise 3
NARRATOR: Number the sentences as you hear them.
CLERK: May I help you?
CUSTOMER: Um. . .I'm looking for some shoes.
CLERK: How about these?
CUSTOMER: Oh, they're too big.
CLERK: Well, how about these?
CUSTOMER: No, they're too small.
CLERK: What about these?
CUSTOMER: Yes, they're fine!

Exercise 4
NARRATOR: Complete the conversations.
    One.
CLERK: May I help you?
CUSTOMER: Yes, I'm looking for some shoes.
CLERK: How about these?
CUSTOMER: They're too small.
CLERK: Or these?
CUSTOMER: Yes. They're perfect.
NARRATOR: Two.
CLERK: May I help you?
CUSTOMER: Yes, I need a hat.
CLERK: How about this?
CUSTOMER: No, it's too big.
CLERK: What about this one?
CUSTOMER: Yes! It's fine.

UNIT 15

What time does Flight 55 arrive?

NARRATOR:	Look at the schedule and listen.
VOICE 1:	Excuse me. What time does Flight 55 arrive?
INFORMATION:	At one twenty.
VOICE 1:	Thank you.
VOICE 2:	When does Flight 54 arrive?
INFORMATION:	Flight 54? Uh, at six forty-five P.M.
VOICE 2:	OK. Thanks.
VOICE 3:	When does Flight 563 arrive?
INFORMATION:	Let's see. Um, at six forty-five P.M.
VOICE 3:	Thanks.
VOICE 4:	What time does Flight 567 arrive?
INFORMATION:	Flight 567? At eleven fifty-five P.M., sir.
VOICE 4:	Thanks a lot.
VOICE 5:	Excuse me. Where does Flight 54 arrive?
INFORMATION:	Where?. . .At Gate 63, ma'am.
VOICE 5:	Thank you.
VOICE 6:	Where does Flight 563 arrive?
INFORMATION:	Flight 563? Um, at Gate 64.
VOICE 6:	OK. Thanks.
VOICE 7:	When does Flight 55 arrive?
INFORMATION:	When? At one twenty.
VOICE 7:	Thanks a lot.
NARRATOR:	Now look at the schedule again and listen.

(Repetition of above)

Exercise 1

NARRATOR:	Listen to the question, look at the schedule, and write the answer.
	One.
VOICE 1:	What time does Flight 563 arrive?
NARRATOR:	Two.
VOICE 2:	Where does Flight 55 arrive?
NARRATOR:	Three.
VOICE 3:	When does Flight 567 arrive?
NARRATOR:	Four.
VOICE 4:	Where does Flight 54 arrive?
NARRATOR:	Five.
VOICE 5:	What time does Flight 55 arrive?
NARRATOR:	Six.
VOICE 6:	When does Flight 54 arrive?
NARRATOR:	Seven.
VOICE 7:	Where does Flight 567 arrive?
NARRATOR:	Eight.
VOICE 8:	When does Flight 563 arrive?
NARRATOR:	Nine.
VOICE 9:	What time does Flight 567 arrive?
NARRATOR:	Ten.
VOICE 10:	Where does Flight 55 arrive?

Exercise 2

NARRATOR:	Number the sentences as you hear them.
VOICE 1:	What time does Flight 55 arrive?
INFORMATION:	At one twenty P.M., ma'am.
VOICE 1:	Thank you.
VOICE 2:	When does Flight 563 arrive?
INFORMATION:	Uh, let's see. At six-forty-five P.M. sir.
VOICE 2:	Thanks.
VOICE 3:	Where does Flight 54 arrive?
INFORMATION:	At Gate 63.
VOICE 3:	Thanks a lot.

Exercise 3

NARRATOR:	Complete the conversations.
	One.
VOICE 1:	Excuse me. What time does Flight 563 arrive?
INFORMATION:	Flight 563? At six forty-five P.M.
VOICE 1:	OK. Thanks.
NARRATOR:	Two.
VOICE 2:	Where does Flight 567 arrive?
INFORMATION:	Flight 567? At Gate 63.
VOICE 2:	Thanks a lot.
NARRATOR:	Three.
VOICE 3:	Excuse me. When does Flight 55 arrive?
INFORMATION:	Let's see. At one twenty P.M.
VOICE 3:	Thank you.

UNIT 16

Where is the 51st Street station?

NARRATOR:	Look at the pictures and listen.
WOMAN:	Excuse me. Where is the 51st Street station?
NARRATOR:	One.
MAN:	Go up the steps.
NARRATOR:	Two.
MAN:	Go straight on, uh, 53rd Street.
NARRATOR:	Three.
MAN:	Then, uh, turn left at First Avenue.
NARRATOR:	Four.
MAN:	And turn right at 51st Street.

NARRATOR: Five.
MAN: Go under the bridge.
NARRATOR: Six.
MAN: And then go down the steps and there's the station.
WOMAN: Thank you very much.
NARRATOR: Now look at the pictures again and listen.

(*Repetition of above, minus the narrator's voice*)

Exercise 1

NARRATOR: Listen to the sentences. Match the sentences with the pictures.

One.
MAN: Go under the bridge.
NARRATOR: Two.
MAN: Go straight.
NARRATOR: Three.
MAN: Turn right.
NARRATOR: Four.
MAN: Go down the steps.
NARRATOR: Five.
MAN: Turn left.
NARRATOR: Six.
MAN: Go up the steps.

Exercise 2

NARRATOR: Put your finger at the bottom of the map on START HERE. Follow the instructions. Then write your answers.

One.
WOMAN: Go straight on Center Avenue. Uh...Turn right at Second Street. Then...turn left at Lincoln Avenue. Go under the bridge....and....turn right at Third Street. Go up the steps on the right.
NARRATOR: Where are you?
NARRATOR: Two.
Put your finger at the bottom of the map and follow the instructions.

MAN: Uh, turn left at First Street. Then, uh, turn right at West Avenue. Go under the bridge.....Go straight to Third Street. Then go under another bridge. And go up the steps.
NARRATOR: Where are you?
NARRATOR: Three.
Put your finger at the bottom of the map and follow the instructions.
WOMAN: Turn right at First Street....Turn left...at Lincoln Avenue. Go straight on Lincoln. Then go under the bridge. Go down the steps, umm, on the left.
NARRATOR: Where are you?
NARRATOR: Four.
Put your finger at the bottom of the map and follow the instructions.
MAN: Umm...Go straight on Center Avenue....and turn left at Second Street. Then, turn left at West Avenue. And go down the steps on the right.
NARRATOR: Where are you?
NARRATOR: Five.
Put your finger at the bottom of the map and follow the instructions.
WOMAN: Go straight on Center Avenue and turn right on Second. At East Avenue, turn left. Go up the steps on the left.
NARRATOR: Where are you?

Exercise 3

NARRATOR: Number the sentences as you hear them.
WOMAN: Excuse me. Where is the 51st Street station?
MAN: Go up the steps.
Go straight on, uh, 53rd Street.
Then, uh, turn left at First Avenue.
And turn right at 51st Street.
Go under the bridge.
And then go down the steps and there's the station.
WOMAN: Thank you very much.

ANSWER KEY

UNIT 1
Ten singles, please.

Exercise 1: 5 7 2 9 8 4 10 6
Exercise 2: 8 2 5 3 9 7 10 1
Exercise 4: six three eight five seven two
Exercise 6: one two three four five six seven eight nine ten

UNIT 2
That's 626-2834.

Exercise 1: 536-4202 345-9752 454-8976 778-2046 626-1139 255-7509 872-3386 871-0482
Exercise 2: 98 15 94 99 40 26 81 55
Exercise 3: 462-8069 332-5178 693-1518 855-4804 771-5178 871-0507 556-2105 988-2720

UNIT 3
Change for a twenty, please.

Exercise 1: 12 16 18 19 17 20 14 11
Exercise 2: 12 15 17 20 11 13 10 18
Exercise 4: sixteen eleven seventeen twelve five nineteen
Exercise 6: eleven twelve thirteen fourteen fifteen sixteen seventeen eighteen nineteen twenty

UNIT 4
Ten tens, please.

Exercise 1: 30 60 14 90 20 11 50 17
Exercise 2: seventy fifteen one hundred eighty forty thirteen sixty eleven
Exercise 4: forty seventeen ninety twelve sixty thirty
Exercise 6: ten twenty thirty forty fifty sixty seventy eighty ninety one hundred

UNIT 5
What's your address?

Exercise 1: 1. 665 State Street 2. 83 East Avenue 3. 428 Pine Street 4. 1404 Spring Road 5. 129 Lake Avenue 6. 5206 Main Street 7. 5790 Elm Street 8. 434 Lincoln Avenue

Exercise 2: 1. 25 2. 54 3. 31 4. 15 5. 04 6. 98 7. 10 8. 02
Exercise 3: 1. 742 2. 1308 3. 625 4. 420 5. 7530 6. 53

UNIT 6
Your name, please.

Exercise 1: 1. i 2. R 3. e 4. d 5. g 6. 1 7. i 8. S 9. g 10. t
Exercise 2: 1. Dine 2. Fenn 3. Gent 4. Leff 5. Keen 6. Teng 7. Finn 8. Stolt
Exercise 3: 1. e 2. w 3. d 4. r 5. g 6. E 7. i 8. l 9. k 10. n
Exercise 4: 1. Ford 2. Low 3. King 4. Gore 5. Niles 6. Soldo 7. Sneed 8. Tewel 9. Lief 10. Denes

UNIT 7
Spell it, please.

Exercise 1: 1. n 2. u 3. Z 4. w 5. V 6. x 7. G 8. y 9. e 10. l
Exercise 2: 1. Bacher 2. Feliz 3. Kohan 4. Chan 5. Barker 6. Moar 7. Gant 8. Major
Exercise 3: 1. p 2. U 3. y 4. M 5. x 6. h 7. v 8. g 9. i 10. z
Exercise 4: 1. James 2. Rubin 3. Paine 4. Quinn 5. Myles 6. Fixx 7. Joyce 8. Brown 9. Velez 10. York

UNIT 8
What would you like to eat?

Exercise 1: 2 6 1 5 3 4
Exercise 2: 5 6 4 2 1 3
Exercise 3: 1. steak, french fries, coffee 2. hamburger, salad, Coke 3. chicken, salad, tea 4. fish, french fries, coffee
Exercise 4: 2 12 5 9 11 1 3 4 8 7 6 10
Exercise 5: 1. salad, Coke 2. hot dog, milk 3. fish, coffee 4. chicken, tea
Exercise 7: 1. chicken 2. french fries 3. coffee 4. sandwich 5. milk 6. hamburger 7. hot dog 8. milkshake 9. tea 10. fish 11. Coke 12. salad 13. water 14. steak

UNIT 9
Tell us about the apartment.

Exercise 1: 2 6 3 4 8 1 7 5
Exercise 2: 1. yes 2. no 3. yes 4. no
5. yes 6. yes 7. no 8. yes
Exercise 3: 5 8 2 1 7 4 6 3 9
Exercise 5: 1. There isn't a kitchen. 2. There's a bedroom. 3. There's a garage. 4. There isn't a balcony. 5. There's a bathroom. 6. There isn't a fireplace. 7. There's a living room. 8. There isn't a dining room.

UNIT 10
I need your name.

Exercise 1: 1. photograph 2. signature 3. phone number 4. check for five dollars 5. name, address 6. check for twenty dollars, photograph 7. signature, photograph 8. check, address, phone number
Exercise 2: 4 5 7 1 8 3 2 6
Exercise 3: 1. b 2. c 3. c 4. a 5. c 6. b

UNIT 11
How much is this shampoo?

Exercise 1: 1. aspirin, $1.35 2. soap, $1.07 3. film, $3.39 4. toothpaste, $2.05 5. shampoo, $1.49 6. aspirin, $2.20
Exercise 2: 2 6 3 1 5 4
Exercise 3: 1. 0 2. 4 3. 0 4. 2 5. 8 6. 1 7. 1 8. 5
Exercise 4: 1. $1.60 2. $2.08 3. $4.15 4. $3.32 5. $1.70 6. $3.79 7. $4.05 8. $1.80 9. $2.19 10. $4.99
Exercise 6: 1. cologne 2. soap 3. shampoo 4. toothpaste 5. film 6. aspirin

UNIT 12
How much are these vitamins?

Exercise 1: 1. razors, 98¢ 2. envelopes, 70¢ 3. pencils, $1.08 4. batteries, 50¢ 5. vitamins, $4.89 6. combs, 98¢
Exercise 2: 1. comb 2. envelope 3. batteries 4. pencil 5. razors 6. battery 7. comb 8. razors 9. pencils 10. envelopes
Exercise 3: 2 7 3 6 8 5 1 4

Exercise 4: 1. vitamins, razor 2. toothpaste, razors 3. soap, combs 4. batteries, comb
Exercise 6: 1. batteries 2. razors 3. combs 4. vitamins 5. envelopes 6. pencils

UNIT 13
Mommy, what are you doing?

Exercise 1: 3 1 2 5 6 4
Exercise 2: 4 3 5 1 6 2 7
Exercise 3: 1. making 2. making, call 3. kissing 4. typing, letter 5. washing, dishes 6. taking, shower
Exercise 4: 1. I'm washing the dishes. 2. I'm typing a letter. 3. I'm taking a shower. 4. I'm kissing Daddy. 5. I'm making a phone call. 6. I'm making hamburgers.

UNIT 14
I'm looking for a hat.

Exercise 1: 1. big hat 2. small shoes 3. hat that fits 4. big hat 5. small shoes 6. hat that fits 7. shoes that fit 8. small shoes
Exercise 2: 4 8 3 2 7 5 6 1
Exercise 3: 1 7 4 2 3 5 6 8
Exercise 4: 1. help, shoes, small, perfect 2. hat, this, too

UNIT 15
What time does Flight 55 arrive?

Exercise 1: 1. at 6:45 P.M. 2. at Gate 63 3. at 11:55 P.M. 4. at Gate 63 5. at 1:20 P.M. 6. at 6:45 P.M. 7. at Gate 63 8. at 6:45 P.M. 9. at 11:55 P.M. 10. at Gate 63
Exercise 2: 8 1 3 5 2 6 4 9 7
Exercise 3: 1. What time, P.M., Thanks 2. Where, arrive, a lot 3. When, Thank you

UNIT 16
Where is the 51st Street station?

Exercise 1: 2 3 4 1 5 6
Exercise 2: 1. At the bank 2. At the shoe store 3. At the lake 4. At the subway 5. At the restaurant
Exercise 3: 6 8 4 1 3 2 5 7
Exercise 5: 1. right 2. under 3. down 4. straight 5. steps 6. Turn